All correspondence to:
www.lovedropsfromheaven.com
or
info@lovedropsfromheaven.com

Acknowledgments

To my wonderful family, Nam, Grace and Hudson.
Nam thanks for proof reading my dyslexic garble, for loving me unconditionally and being a man who truly models the strength and humility of Christ. Kids, thank you for making the dinner and not killing each other while I was typing and all the other things which are too many to list… love you guys, can't believe you're mine and soooo normal!

Thanks Claire for shining so brightly that you warm the atmosphere with your infectious love and make a way for the rest of us to shine. You're an inspiration!

Directions for use!

These Love drops are designed to be used as a pick me up, like a spiritual vitamin supplement. One a day should give you plenty to chew on and hopefully nourish your soul. There's a 3 month supply here so bless yourself, chew slowly and enjoy babe! You are amazing…

Love Ruth x

Contents

Drop 1 ~ Loved

Girlfriend you are one loved woman! You are the object of someone's affection, did you know that? You are a 'Princess' chosen by the Almighty God of heaven and earth... He looked down into the pages of time, went weak at the knees, did back flips when He saw you and guess what? Out of all the millions of people on this earth, He chose you! To Him when you smile, it is like a magnificent beam of sunshine breaking through the grey. No other love meets the criteria that ***you*** meet; you are uniquely shaped for the embrace in His heart. When you talk to Him, there's a hush in heaven's singing because the beloved of the Lord speaks.[1] You are the priority in His day, the song in His daydream and the pain of His longing. Girlfriend you are one loved woman…

Your lover trusts His dreams to you. His hopes He scatters as petals before you to fragrance your world because He loves you. *Only, sometimes you don't see them.* He perseveres even through the pain of rejection when your love for Him grows cool. He will never lie to you or leave you. He will fight for you, protect you… write love songs for you[2]… He died for you. Girlfriend, you are one loved woman…

You see, we were on a runaway train to hell because of our sin, but Jesus loved us so much He made a way of rescue for us. Now He is the one who swoops in through the castle window on a burning rope and saves you from the place of your imprisonment. He is faithful and will never let you down – ever. When you're flustered, premenstrual, in a tizz, He is the one who, if you allow Him, will soothe your soul and give you peace.[3]

Just take a moment – how wonderful to be the centre of someone's world, particularly when that person is the King of Kings.

Psalm 73 v 25 *"Whom have I in heaven but you? Since I have you what else on earth could I desire beside you?"*

Go look up the scriptures below and be blessed…

[1] Rev 8 v 1
[2] 1 Cor 13 v 4 – 8
[3] John 14 v 27

Drop 2 ~ Wonderful you

I am actually a very forgetful person; I have been known to misplace our youngest child. I've put a bottle of shampoo in the door of the fridge instead of the milk and last year, I forgot how many years I'd been married…Doh! I'm also a bit of a rottweiler the week before my period and when I get too tired I cry, a lot!

But here's what's cool, God is ok with all of 'my stuff', He made me that way and can work around the dippiness, even the ugliness of my character. Actually for a long time I wanted to be one of these "in control, power filled, kick ass, quotable, scarily together women of God." But after years of trying, I've come to realise that try as I might to perfect myself, I've got to be me. …Amazingly that's exactly who God wants me to be ….. Well "Duhhh!" you could say and you'd be right…

Girlfriend that's who God wants you to be…Just you! Wonderful You![1]

We've all got strengths and weaknesses. Sometimes God is gracious and we do and say wise things; sometimes we will come out with quotable stuff; but the truth is that even if I take my son to the vets and the cat to Karate, my God is firing moments of greatness through me because He's at work in me,[2] and in spite of me... How mind blowing is that?

Be encouraged today if you're willing, God wants to fire up His creativity and He spins around you[3] shaping something incredible out of the raw material that is you. All that you have to do is live each moment totally for Him.

You Rock!

[1] Psalm 139 v 14
[2] 1 John 4 v 4

[3] Zephaniah 3 v 17 *"The Lord your God is with you. He is mighty to save, He will take great delight in you. He will quiet you with His love. He will rejoice over you with singing."*

Drop 3 ~ Dare to dream

When was the last time you took time to be still…to simply dream and ponder? Life can overtake us and it's easy to forget to take time to just chill and think happy thoughts. I know for some of you reading this the only time you get a place to think is when you're using the loo, but hey, there's no rule that says great dreams aren't formulated in small places. In fact, I'm sure there's a proverb backing that up somewhere!

The point is it doesn't matter where you dream, but rather that you just dare to do it – Dream! I believe God puts dreams on our hearts.[1] Our God loves to watch us have a total blast as we live out the journey that is this life. Remember the foundation of all He does is His passionate love for you, princess! He places dreams on your heart in order for Him to give you the desires of your heart.

Have you a special secret desire, which causes you to smile with hope and anticipation on the inside when you think about it? What's your happy thought right now? Are there thoughts buzzin' in and out of your heart's flow? (If you can't think of one give yourself a hug… and possibly chocolate and snuggle with God till He reminds you.) *Word of wisdom: exhaustion is the biggest dream thief and joy stealer I know! If you feel like you're in a hole, sleep can give you strength for the climb out.*[2]

Princess, God wants us to have dreams; He wants to watch like a parent on Christmas morning as you unpack His promises over your life. He wants to cheer lead as you make that change, have that rest, climb out of that rut, stop that attitude or whatever is holding you back. It's up to you to set the wheels in motion to make your dreams your reality. What would it take for you to start that process? Why not take 5, switch off the telly and list some of your dreams. Pray over them and watch your Heavenly Dad over the coming months answer your prayers.

Joel 2 v 28 - *"I will pour out my Spirit on all people. Your sons and daughters will prophesy, your old men will dream dreams and your young men/women will see visions."*

[1] Proverbs 37 v 4
[2] Isaiah 40 v 29

Drop 4 ~ Glory goal!

We can get ourselves so tied up in knots can't we? Lose our focus and make loving God complicated when its not. When you fall in love the one thing you want to do is please the object of your love and so you try and please them. You focus on them and their desires with tunnel vision. Don Miller in his book 'Blue Like Jazz' describes falling in love as a taste of heaven on earth because you live totally for the other person. Your goal is to lift them, cherish them and do them good.[1] Actually over the years that has become my litmus test in 'Christian circles'. If something or someone is grabbing the focus towards themselves and off God I tend to question the authenticity of what they're about.

Our goal on a very simple level is to lift the focus to Glorify God above all else. The flowers do it, the bees do it, even educated peas do it… (*or something like that*) they all bring Glory to their creator.[2] Keeping God glorified in my world is my prime objective. We can glorify Him in what we don't say! We can glorify Him by using our energy and money to bless others; or by being honest about ourselves and not trying to keep up our prideful pretensions…

What's really cool is that glorifying God isn't always something we 'do' but it's kind of who we are.[3] Simply put, we are made to reflect His glory. There will be areas which are dulled through our own selfishness but God has promised us help with the polishing process. He is a perfectionist when it comes to shining us up and he will complete the job… If we can work with Him, by simply making it our goal each day to please the lover of our lives, we can only but bring Glory! Phew what a relief…Keep it simple babes x.

*Take some time to think about the smudges on the window of your soul. Ask God to help you buff 'em till He's glorified in those places too!

Luke 2 v 14 – *"Glory to God in the highest and peace to his people on whom His favour rests."*

[1] Blue Like Jazz by Donald Miller ch.14 pg 151, Thomas Nelson, Inc.
[2] Genesis 1 v 20 - 25
[3] Genesis 1 v 27

Drop 5 ~ Get your booty moving

Obstacles are the things you see when you take your eyes off the goal!!

It's easier to direct a moving object than a stationary one. But sometimes it's hard to get started isn't it…? I know in my life God has mostly required me to make the first move before He starts directing my steps. It's a bit scary at first but it's grand because every time He is faithful. He rarely comes through with the solutions we think of… He's far too creative for that. I guess He wants us to grow in the process, so He uses our baby steps of faith to encourage and inspire us.

So sweet cheeks…what do you need to move your booty on…?

The world would dictate that money, fame or some other form of self satisfaction are worthy of your time and pain! But consider… what is the point of having a goal unless it has life in it?[1] Girls sometimes we chase after the candyfloss of life which isn't really life. Sure it's sweet, fluffy and pink and seems like fun but when you bite into it, it's without substance and it'll rot your teeth! If you're going to spend your time and energy on something ask yourself does it have substance, will it glorify God, and will it be bursting with life?

To find your goal start by looking at what's in your hands right now, what things has the Lord given you stewardship over? Once you've identified your goal – go for it. It may take hard work and perseverance but then things of great value come with a price. Don't let set-backs rob your vision. Even the Wright Brothers took over a hundred attempts before they got anything to fly. You have awesome purpose and joy unspeakable before you.

"Commit to the Lord whatever you do and yours plans will succeed."[2]

Girlfriend you're on to a winner because when you're committed to doing things Gods way your plans (only if they're holy, ha ha) will succeed…

Halleluiah!! *Thought food:* Your priority is what you are giving your time to right now… What are you spending your time doing? Are there changes you need to make so you can get your teeth stuck into the 'meat' of life?

Mathew 6 v 33 - *"But seek first the kingdom of God and His righteousness, and all these things will be given to you as well."*

[1]Deuteronomy 30 v 19
[2] Proverbs 16 v 3

Drop 6 ~ Be extraordinary

I've been really gripped by the vulnerability of the method Jesus Christ chose to enter this world. The sheer ordinariness of it...[1]

Jesus could have come to earth in a million fantastic ways, but no... He chose the most humble, most vulnerable, most ordinary of ordinary ways! It so rocks that the Supreme Being, the indescribable power source of perfect love came in the way that He did. It really encourages me because I am often intimidated by the in-your-face-ness of our fame fuelled culture, where the things which are flashiest and loudest get attention. When I'm feeling pretty insignificant I find it comforting to think about how my precious Jesus chose the ordinary over the glitz.

Do you know He chose to spend His eternity with you over the splendour of the angels and Heavenly beings? He delights in you at every moment of who you are. Consider this for a moment... how much more vulnerable is God's position in this relationship with us? He will never walk away, He is forever faithful but we know this is not true of us...

Perhaps it's when we're at our most vulnerable that God is at His most spectacular in our journey.[2] We are all vulnerable in different areas...But we have the certainty of a faithful God and the comfort of knowing when we feel really small He is huge and sovereign.[3]

Choose to look for the extra-ordinariness of Jesus in the ordinariness of this day. Don't worry about feeling vulnerable before God; that's a good place to be because the reality is He's chosen to be the more vulnerable to us.

Ephesians 4 v 20-21 *"Now to Him who is able to do immeasurably more than we could ask or imagine, according to His power that is at work in us, to Him be the glory in the church and in Christ Jesus throughout all generations for ever and ever Amen!"*

[1] Matthew 1 v 18-25
[2] 2 Corinthians 12 v 8-12
[3] Daniel 7 v 27

Drop 7 ~ Are you willing?

In Exodus 35 the Israelite people finally get it… they finally yield and submit their will to the will of God. They stand together with one purpose (to see the temple of the Lord established). As I was reading this something struck me…

- V21 and everyone who was **willing** and whose heart was moved came and brought an offering to the Lord.
- V26 and all the women who were **willing** and had the skill spun the goat hair *for the garments of the temple.*
- V29 all the Israelite men and women who were **willing** brought freewill offerings to the Lord.
- Ch. 36 v 2 and every skilled person whom the Lord had given the ability and who was **willing** came to do the work…

Are you getting the recurring theme through this? These people were willing!!! God doesn't force us to do things His way… that's why we have the free will thing going on. However, He is so totally nuts in love with us that He simply wants the very best for us and that, simply put, is His will. He sees the big long term picture of your life and even if something awful is unfolding in your world today, you can know that when it's surrendered to Him it will bring forth life in the fullness of time.[1]

Honey bun, life just won't work until we get a willing heart[2]… ouch! Sometimes the truth clashes with my 'I wanna do it my way' attitude…! But here's the deal; as we grow up in trusting God we see again and again how He works for our good. The other brill thing about keeping willingness in our spirit is that it keeps us open to His leading, and His awesome plans and purpose.[3]

What are you holding on to? Why not dare to trust the outcome to the one who loves you the most?

2 Corinthians 8 v 11 - *"Now finish the work, so that your eager willingness to do it may be matched by your completion of it according to your means. For if the willingness is there, the gift is acceptable according to what one has, not according to what he does not have."*

[1] John 12 v 24
[2] Psalm 51 v 10-12
[3] Jeremiah 29 v 11-13

Drop 8 ~ Burn, baby, burn!

What burns within you… and I don't mean last night's curry! What rings your bell or floats your boat?

I remember the first time I heard my voice as I sang at the bottom of a stairwell; it sent a shiver up my spine and into the heavens. In that moment I knew song would be part of me for the rest of my life. I love singing…When I have the luxury of an empty house I still sing my head off and dance around the kitchen like a mad woman! Often God gives us a passion or a fire within the core of our being which flares up and causes a spark and we know eternity is sown into that ignition moment.

One little spark can start a roaring fire, girl we need to encourage one another, stir up the fire of our souls.[1] It's incredibly important that we cheerlead each other as we mission to this world so that we burn hot and bright. When we're fired up we, just like fire, are powerful, dangerous, and brilliant for our King. BUT "and it's a big one" as the man says, fire is only useful when under control… Precious sister, we need to have our passions under the control of the Holy Spirit[2] so that we're led by Him to flow in the right direction. It's good to get all fired up about serving God or fighting the injustices in our world but if we are going to be effective and useful to the Kingdom we need to allow God to channel our passions. If we're all fired up but not under the control of the Holy Spirit we can go off in an unholy tangent which ends up burning and hurting rather than causing life.

I believe those things that burn or fire us up are inspired by the Holy Spirit in prayer and preparation. I want to encourage you to place your heart into God's eternal flame and get fired up with vision for your life. Today, ask your Father to show you the passions He has placed in you, celebrate your journey thus far… you have an exciting future ahead of you.[3] If your fire's gone cold - go get near some one who's hot. Pray with them learn from them, till you heat up. Now go write a card, send some flowers or pick up the phone and cheerlead someone who has been a fire stoker in your world.

Luke 12 v 34 "*For where your treasure is there your heart will be also.*"

[1] Hebrews 12 v 1-3
[2] Romans 8 v 6
[3] Psalm 37 v 37

Drop 9 ~ Gifts from above

Once upon a time there was a child who was journeying through life in the world with her lovely mum. The mother loved the child with such love and, born from this love, she gave her child a rare and precious gift.

It was beautifully wrapped in gold tissue paper with a gorgeous bow around the huge box. The child, even though she trusted and loved her mother, had a weird feeling about the gift. She felt somehow afraid that what was inside the gift box was strange and unfamiliar. So the box was set aside and remained unopened for a long time.

The girl went through life and had many ups and downs as we all do. Many times she wished for things in herself that would aid her in her journey. Eventually she grew old and on her deathbed remembered the gift box given to her by her beloved mother a lifetime before and so she asked her family to fetch it. All eyes were on the old woman as she opened the box.... She reached in a lifted out precious stones, each one unique in its intensity and brilliance...

The first one, was breath-taking in its radiance, colour and shape, it had the word ***Love*** magnificently engraved on it. The old lady remembered all the moments in her life when she felt unloved, she remembered the times in her life when she had hardened her heart and vowed she'd never love again... And something like a love's first kiss brushed her lips.

The next stone said ***Grace***; it was exceptional in cut and class and she remembered all the times she'd beaten herself up because of stupid mistakes... And the burdens she was never meant to carry slid to the floor and disappeared. The next stone was ***Hope***; it looked special and magnifying when gazed upon. She remembered days when she gave permission to despair to take up residence in her heart... And something like the sound of distant singing and the fragrance of wild flowers floated into the room.

The next stone was ***Peace;*** it was large, clear and made the room dance with light as she held it up. She felt a deeply satisfying glow inside her. She lifted another; it said, ***Courage***. This one was solid and deep and as she held it she felt a surge of strength shoot through her and all her fears depart. The last gift was ***Eternal Life*** and the woman felt a joy unspeakable enfold her in its arms and soothe her soul....[1] and it was then, as a fleeting thought she wondered why she'd not opened the box when it was there all along, but then, it didn't matter now...

Princess, God tells us that He will equip us for all He calls us to do in this life.[2] He promises never to leave or forsake us.[3] He has left us the ultimate comfort blanket in His Holy Spirit[4] and if we are willing, He has treasures from heaven for us to unpack in the fullness of time to equip us as we journey through life.

Sweetheart, are you going to open your box or just look at it?

[1] 1 John 5 v 13
[2] Hebrews 13 v 20-21 [3] Hebrews 13 v 5 / Deut 31 v 6 [4] John 14 v 16-18

Drop 10 ~ Hold out for the best

We so think we know what's good for us and what's going to bring us joy in our lives, and hey a lot of the time we're right. We need exercise to stay healthy, we need sleep to be rested, we need friends to give us a sense of companionship and belonging and all that sort of thing.

There are however, many times when what I've thought was good for me simply wasn't! You know what I'm talking about… that extra glass of wine or slice of double chocolate pudding, pushing myself even when I know I'm already exhausted, or having a rant about someone who's ticked me off in the day. Ever done any of that? Ever entered into a relationship or a job that you knew deep down was wrong for you, with disastrous results? The truth is we all have, babe, and that's why we need God to guide us in each moment of each day.

I've learned in life that poor choices need to be defended with excuses. So we'll excuse our irritability because we're stressed or our ungodly exhaustion because its 'ministry'. But the truth is grumpiness isn't ok nor is exhaustion. I know there will be those of you who are reading this who are totally knackered because that's the season you're in, but constant exhaustion is not the big plan for your life because God wants you to have a good life, believe me… Ask yourself what you can change in your world to get the best and hold out for it. This may mean you have to ask for respect from your kids or wait on the Lord when making big choices. It may mean you listen to trusted godly friends when they're warning you about a course of action. Babe, you deserve the best and sometimes that will require self-discipline in order for you to not settle for a quick fix.

When making choices the converse works too because good choices need no defence. Choosing to stop after that second glass of wine doesn't need defending. Choosing to switch off an unholy film or stay in a difficult place and walk in obedience rather than walk away simply needs no defence; good choices stand up to any argument.

The devil wants us to settle for 'good enough' or a short term 'fix' which will bring forth a rubbish result - but the Father, your Father wants his children to have the best.[1] Getting the best often takes time and patience. You see, it takes courage not to walk away when the situation seems hopeless; it takes discipline and strength of character… in short getting the best doesn't come easy or cheap.[2] But that's exactly why its worth sticking out the short term pain of today…the long-term gain of tomorrow will far outweigh everything you're going through in the pain of today's moment… God says He'll help us, He wants the best for us for the long term, not a cheap imitation.

Just wait and see… the best is yet to come, just keep taking those wee steps of righteousness in each moment of your day and your Father will do the rest. Princess, it's a promise…

Philippians 3 v 14 - *"I press on towards the goal to win the prize for which God has called me heavenwards in Christ Jesus."*

[1] Psalm 84 v 4-5
[2] Hebrews 12 v 1

Drop 11 ~ Count your blessings

Comparisons can work both ways can't they…we can see what we don't have rather than what we've got. A good friend of mine became ill recently and as a consequence had to undergo many embarrassing tests. I really cringed as she recalled the events of her treatment and it made me appreciate my own good health. It struck me, as I was pondering, how much I have in my world to be really very thankful for.

Often we have the best blessings in loads of areas but we simply can't see them. Life takes over, appointments get made, dinners get cooked, squabbles get sorted…and somewhere in the mist that can be our busy lives we lose sight of the awesome privilege of human life. We probably have the certainty of our next meal, or a comfortable place to sit down upon to read this book. We may have people who care for us and differing positions or roles which fulfil us and these are good things, yes blessings.

You see honey bun, comparing our lives or thighs or whatever puts a filter over our focus. Comparing takes us into either pride or dissatisfaction; neither shows anything in a good way. The truth is there will always be people better off, better looking, less screwed up than you but there'll also be people far worse off. It's all a matter of comparison. It is well documented within psychology that here in western civilisation where we have so much, we are the least satisfied. Are you dissatisfied and held back because of what you don't have? What positive things can you be thankful for right now? I really do believe we can train our knee jerk response to focus on the positives. Even in the midst of awful situations.

I'll give you a couple of examples…When I found out the lump in my breast was cancer I was honestly able to rejoice that I had…
1) a wonderfully loving yet nutty family, 2) that I had access to treatment, 3) for the tulip bulbs which came up in my garden and surprised me, 4) that to my closest friends I'm now known as wonkey donkey and find it really funny and, lastly 5) for my husband who, incidentally still thinks I'm hot! *Bless Him!* Start today and train yourself to search out the hidden treasures of blessing that are right under your nose?

List five things that you can be thankful for right now… And know you are a beautiful, blessed, loved, valued, chosen child of God. I thank God for –YOU!

Phil 4 v 4 - *"Rejoice in the Lord always and again, girlfriend, I say rejoice!"*

Drop 12 ~ <u>Cinderella time</u>

Once upon a time there was a little princess who was unhappy. She looked at her glamorous princess friends and thought to herself, "If only I could be more like them I would be happy." They looked so confident being the daughters of Kings and all… however the Princess still felt unhappy being her and wished she was someone else… "Aw!!! I wish I was someone else," she sighed.

Suddenly there was a large Poof! And standing there before her was a beautiful fairy. **"I am your fairy godmother,"** she said. "I will grant your wish, walk a day in another person's shoes and see how that is." So the princess did but they were big and clumpy and she kept falling over… "These are no good," she said, "have you anything else?" "MMMM, let me see," said the fairy godmother, and she took out another pair of shoes. As the princess tried to walk in these shoes she found them far too small, they cut into her ankles and made them bleed!
"These are no good either", she wailed. Box after box was opened; the princess tried on many different people's shoes that day but nothing was a good fit. The princess was still unhappy…

Just then a handsome prince came riding by… and stopped, noticing the damsel in distress!!! Being the practical type of guy that he was, he said, "Why don't you try those shoes?" pointing to the princess's own shoes. "In fact as I'm soooo very handsome and dashing, allow me little lady." At which point the princess threw up! Oh no, only joking as she was a respectable princess she allowed her feet to be shod appropriately. When she recovered her composure she found these shoes, her own shoes were the best. In fact she could run, dance, jump and walk beautifully *in her own shoes.*

The moral… You are made the way you are because God designed it so.[1] By being true to yourself in your weaknesses as well as your strengths you will fit perfectly into the tailor made plan for you life, which God has prepared for you even before you were born.[2]

God has things <u>only you</u> can do… are you wearing the right shoes for the race he has called <u>you</u> to run or are you doing the marathon of life in someone else's stilettos? OUCH!

Girlfriend be true to yourself, love yourself and rest secure in what it says in Ephesians 2 v 10 *"For we are God's workmanship, created in Christ Jesus to do good works, which He has prepared in advance for us to do."*

Now slip on those sling backs, lace those boots or pull up your Ugg's or whatever you're wearing, but let's do this thang!

[1] Psalm 139 v 13-16
[2] Jeremiah 29 v 11

Drop 13 ~ Confrontation: Argh!

Am I the only one who'd run a marathon, or have a bikini wax rather than confront someone? I hate it…and yet there's something very healing and uniting when confrontation is undertaken in a God glorifying way. I believe we can do a great disservice to a brother or sister when we are too cowardly to confront a situation. I had a situation once where I had to muster all the courage I could and talk over a behaviour pattern with one of my team which really troubled me. When we'd talked it through it turned out she was unaware of her actions and to her credit was gracious enough to take the correction. As a result of her good attitude and her humility we grew stronger in our relationship.

God wants us to walk in love and truth… so why are we Christians so bad at that? Why don't we lovingly say when there's a bogie in a nostril, or parsley in teeth? Could it be because in the first instance we've not invested sufficient love and time building our relationships? When you know you're loved you can take a challenging word, because you know the motive is to build you up not tear you down. When we invest in people and they are secure in the knowledge that we love them a loving openness is the result.

It tells us in Ephesians that we war not with flesh and blood i.e. People! Rather the powers and principalities manipulating and seducing the pawns or people involved.[1] When we see the situation (and how Satan often works in it) as ***the enemy*** and not the person, it makes room for God's AGAPE[2] love. When we're looking to God it gives a renewed sense of direction in our prayers for the other party. It protects us in that we are not focused on the person/problem but on the solution. It is an amazing thing to experience God's Love stirring up within you for a person who has deeply wronged you.

So often we smile through gritted teeth rather than speak a loving truth. Why? Love always protects… so it's unloving to smile rather than say, "Hang on babe, you know I love you and it's because I love you I think you should have a rethink." So even when one of my girlfriends with a string of broken relationships tells me she's found Mr. Right again and has signed over the deeds to her house… if I love her as I'm supposed to,[3] my role is to confront her with the love that will not wave her over the edge of yet another cliff! Then commit myself to loving her through whatever mess she may or may not get herself into.

Of course we carry a responsibility with truth because it must always be spoken for the edification of another. We are in the creation business not destruction! I have found when I've really prayed over a period of time one of two things happen… a) the person and their problem gets dealt with by God or b) when I do speak God sets it up in both of our hearts. God seldom rushes; we shouldn't either particularly with confrontation. Ask yourself, are there relationships you need to pray God's AGAPE love into? How can you bring glory into issues rather than running away from them or pretending they don't exist?

[1] Ephesians 6 v 12
[2] Ephesians 3 v 16-19
[3] 1Corinthians 13 v 1-7 & John 13 v 34-35

Drop 14 ~ Forgiveness

I thought it would be practical to write about forgiveness after writing about confrontation! Ha ha…

One of my heroes is Corrie Ten Boom, she was a POW in the 2nd World War; she went through awful atrocities in a German concentration camp and wrote a *real* book called 'The Hiding Place'. Awesome read if you get the chance. Anyway she was speaking in America when one of the Nazi guards who'd abused her came up and asked her to forgive him and right then and there she chose to! The thing is, she was confronted with a situation of choice which is exactly what forgiveness is – a choice.

One thing in life that's sure is at some point we are going to be hurt or offended. We can choose to embark on the process of forgiveness and ask God for the supernatural ability to move forward and let go of the offence. Hunny bun, I've had to forgive some awful things and I'm not saying this is at all easy. When you've been deeply hurt or betrayed forgiveness has to be a choice followed by the action of ongoing forgiveness. It's a process of walking your choice out in the moments when the sting of hurt tries to crawl back into your soul. Many times I've caught myself stewing in a sense of injustice and reliving the event. Ever done that or is this just me? I've had to repent of picking up the very thing I'd set down at the foot of the cross!

By walking out the obedience of forgiveness we assume the proactive position of bringing closure to the past. One of my favourite Bible teachers, Beth Moore, sums up the potential of forgiveness where she explains, "The Greek word for forgiveness is *aphieme.* It means, 'to let go from one's power, possession, to let go free, let escape'. She points out the irony in that un-forgiveness is "the means by which we securely bind ourselves to that which we hate the most".[1] We've all got to forgive, there's no opt out clause for the especially wounded.[2] This is REAL Christianity!

You see we've all been wounded and have caused wounds, this is the sad reality. We shouldn't be surprised when we have to follow Christ's example, we should expect it. Girlfriend no matter what befalls us it will never be to the point of pain in the same way as Jesus experienced it. Because God loves us so much He doesn't want us to carry unnecessary burdens of bitterness through life; that's exhausting! Sweetheart you are so loved, don't stay trapped and bound up by the pain of the past. You have the power to release yourself today.

Today I want to encourage you to spend some time with the Lord and allow Him to reveal what is holding you back, so that you can be free. If you're struggling to forgive – cut the weight off your back…right now repent and ask God to help you as you walk your decision out. How fresh, how empowering is that? You Go Girl!
"God can mend a broken heart, but He needs all the pieces" (Bumper sticker)

A footnote: trust and forgiveness are two very different things. If your trust has been broken, you'd do well to forgive and allow time to prove a person or a situation's trustworthiness.[3]

[1] Beth Moore 'Living Beyond Yourself' pg.127 Life Way Press 2005
[2] Luke 11 v 4 -3 & Matthew 11 v 9

Drop 15 ~ That's m' boy

1 Corinthians 10 v 31 *"Whatever you do, do it all to the glory of God."*

Do you know your Father's heart just swells with pride when He looks at you?

The other day I was feeling rough… like I was coming down with something but I needed to get some shopping, there was NOTHING in the house. You know those times when you look in the fridge and decide marmalade on a tomato just won't work? The children were still off school for the summer hols and I knew I'd have to take our little boy with me. I crawled out of bed and explained to him that mummy was feeling yuck and he needed to behave himself and be helpful in the supermarket.

We parked and got out and my wee son sprang into superman/ knight in shining armour/ prince charming mode, all rolled into one!!!
He got a trolley and wouldn't allow me to push it…
He went to the shelf and gradually filled the trolley…
He even offered to sign my debit card!! I felt such a surge of pride watching him struggle to reach the high shelves and push the trolley, which was enormous, compared to him.

As I watched him I thought about how I do things for God. None of us have great finesse with the shopping cart of life; three wheels always go in different directions! We will wobble our trolley through life and sometimes mistake the stuff we put into it, like washing powder instead of pasta. God is cool for us to get it mixed up. He's bigger than our muddles and totally able to cover them. When we steer life the wrong way or life goes all wonkey and we sometimes bump into people EEK! He can work all things to good for those who are called according to His good plan and purpose.[1] Doesn't that bless you?

Just like my little boy we may not do the job with great finesse or in extra quick and efficient time BUT… I just know my Father is blessed when the attitude of my heart simply wants to please Him. I wonder why we struggle to do everything to the standard of perfection when all God wants is *our* best.

Be encouraged to do the best for your father to YOUR ability with your heart set on lovingly serving[2]…. And do you know I have a hunch your father will be looking at you and telling the angels…Dat's ma child!!!

Why not look up the scripture references below and give yourself some sugar from your God today.

[1] Romans 8 v 28

[2] Ephesians 6 v 7 -8 *"Serve wholeheartedly as if you are serving the Lord, not men, because you know that the Lord will reward everyone for whatever good he does, whether he is a slave or free."*

Drop 16 ~ Dead heading the daisies

I love gardening, I love to water my garden at night and smell the oriental lilies and the night scented stock. I love the coolness and stillness of the garden at twilight, there is a real sense of peace. It's so wonderful to put a seed in the ground and watch it grow into something fragrant and beautiful. Do you know we can grow the garden of our souls? We can give our Father joy at the blossoms we produce there as the fragrance wafts up to Him.

I know this is a well used analogy...... It's good to make sure we are rooting in the right compost; it's great to drink the water of life from the spirit and it's wonderful to bask in the light of God's glory. BUT... you knew there was a buttttt coming didn't you...! I was mulling all this over as I was dead heading my daisies; I'd just come back from a conference.... I was all on fire and feeling really like go get 'em tiger! And like oh! I so want to be mature and reach new heights of holiness and righteousness and..... and... and... and......... God spoke to me...

If I really want to bloom to keep producing fresh blossoms of revelation we need to dead head the areas of our lives that are not producing any more...So often God pulls me up short, eh? Jenny Gilpin said, "We can't rely on past victories for today's revelation."[1]

We are only as good as the stuff growing and alive in us today. How often have you heard someone tell and retell the story of past achievements? You know what I mean...the glory days. I want to be living new achievements everyday. Ask yourself what are you growing today? When was the last time you felt a sense of achievement? When was the last time you felt inspired?

It's a good thing to enjoy the garden of your life, to take the time to appreciate who you're planted beside and enjoy the colours and perfumes. But boring old maintenance is required if growth is to be encouraged.

You see, dead heading flowers isn't completely necessary. The plant will still produce flowers.... But you won't get the best out of it. It will simply get by. I don't want to just get by... Do you? I want to live life in a big full on, full-blossomed, smelly, life filled and abundant way! When you cut away the dead heads you make room for new growth and further blossoms. You encourage the plant to mature and become stronger. Sometimes it's not the right season for a full on cut back to ground level pruning; it may be all that's in order for you to get the best from the season you're in, is a bit of dead heading. Anyway you awesome woman of God, ask yourself, what's producing life in you today? Do you need to deadhead a few daisies or fertilise your roots?

You've got homework today but it will totally bless you ...Go look up John 15 1-8 to catch my drift.... X

[1] Jenny Gilpin quoted at 'Fabulous You Conference' Hope city Church, Bernard Road, Sheffield 2003.

Drop 17 ~ Declare the truth

God tells us in the Bible that His will for us is to live in freedom and walk in the truth of knowing Him. John 8 v 31 *"If you hold on to my teaching, you are really my disciples. Then you will know the truth, and the truth will set you free."* Have you ever thought what it is you need to be freed from?

You see, most of us don't live in actual prisons or under house arrest, or wear shackles do we? No, our prisons are much more subtle. We are bound up with past hurts which keep us locked in depression, with disappointments when our reality clashes with our idealistic dreams. We're enfolded in disillusionment when our leaders show us they're just as flawed as the rest of humanity. We're paralyzed by insecurities and fears and drown in hopelessness when we get it wrong, again. I'm thinking perhaps there's a lot we need to be freed from. Hmmm...?

When you feel like the world is pressing in on you read these truths out loud. Truth is like a weapon, a pistol which you can whip out to defeat all those negative thoughts which try to overwhelm you and take you captive.

Are you ready? Take aim.... Fire!

1. You are loved completely. (Romans 5 v 8)
2. You are accepted and loved by God, but He loves us just as we are, works in progress. (John 15 v 19)
3. You are God's own children. (Eph 1v 5)
4. You have power and authority over Satan because you belong to God. (James 4 v 7)
5. You are going to be with Jesus one day and it's going to be brill! (2 Cor 5 v 1)

OK and here are some truths about God that too often we forget...

6. God the Father has paid the price for our sin by sacrificing *His* beloved child. (Romans 5 v 8)
7. The Holy Spirit of God lives in us helping us, we're not on our own with all the 'stuff' of life. (Acts 2 v 17-21)
8. God is faithful and constant in His love, it never changes. (Isaiah 41 v 7)
9. God is worthy of all glory and honour just because He is who He is. (Rev 4 v 8)

10. God always wants the very best for us. (Phil 1 v 9)

Beautiful child of God, this is your day, nothing can hold you back. Declare the truth regardless of how you feel....Break out and be free!

Galatians 5 v 1 *"It is for freedom that Christ has set us free. Stand firm then and do not let yourselves be burdened again..."*

Drop 18 ~ What's in a name?

In the Arabic culture people have a formal name that they are known by and another name known only by very close family members and friends. This is an acknowledgement of the depth of relationship and how intimate the knowledge of that person is. If you know their 'name' then you really *know* them, as the name sums up their character or identity. I suppose the nearest thing we have in our culture to this is a pet name or nick-name to denote a closeness of relationship.

Think about some of the names you've been called in life so far and the relationship to the title and the knowledge of who you are. I betcha there are some you like and some you hate! You may have been labelled in the playground or other social group; perhaps in your family you had a pet name. We often live up or down to the names we are called…Do you know our wonderful God has some names for you? Yes He calls you His beloved, His precious child, Princess of the kingdom of heaven, child of light and many more! All of the names He has for you are wrought in love and a deeper knowledge of you than you have of yourself! You are so very precious that special names are spoken over you in heavenly places.

Our God has names for himself too… Provider, Healer, Defender, Forerunner and Finisher, Friend and Saviour, lots more, but in short, Name above all Names! Each one shows us the faithful never changing totally perfect character of the great 'I AM'.

Beloved, your God wants to be close to you, He wants to be known deeply by you and so He has given us His name…'I am'. God knew you before time was set in place. Before you were knit together in your mother's womb He chose you and set His desire and favour on you.[1] He tells us "I have called you by name and you are mine." How wonderful to be named, known and cherished by the creator of the universe? And know that your name is written in His book of eternal life![2]

Song of Songs 1 v 3 "*…Your name is like perfume poured out… fragrant and pleasing."*

[1] Psalm 139 v 13
[2] Hebrews 12 v 22-24

Drop 19 ~ Don't rain on my parade

The other night as I was washing up I looked out the kitchen window. *Nothing exciting there then!* It had been a glorious sunny day… you know the sort where the kids run around in their knickers and you have lunch outside. Anyway my daughter and her friend had been messing about with the hose and had sprayed the windows at the back of the house. It really looked as though it had rained. For some reason I felt a wee twinge of sadness that the nice sunny day was over and yet I knew the reality was that it hadn't rained. It was just that the windows were wet. I know, how dippy am I? God spoke to me and said don't be fooled by what you think you see. Don't rain on my parade of this day.

So often we can see some wonderful creation and still get the wrong picture. You see one of the tactics of the enemy is to distort our perspective just enough to fool us and throw us off beam. Right now you are walking in the middle of an awesome tailor made plan. Don't let water on the glass fool you into thinking this life, your life, isn't amazing…It is!

YOU are full of purpose and potential; you are still undiscovered in so many areas. Yes you are a work in progress, we all are, but don't be robbed of the wonder of what God can do in and through you. Refuse to let the enemy rain on the parade of your life. It's your life not his, which is what maddens him so much! He's blown his chance, don't allow him to influence yours…don't let your enemy rob you princess. Stand up tall and humble and trust God works EVERYTHING to the good of those who love Him and are called according to His good plan and purpose.[1]

As we march in righteousness, our wonderful Jesus is our greatest cheerleader. As we break through strongholds and comfort zones, He is shouting you can do it! You are no accident… choose today to march onward and upward in the peace of knowing you are being shaped and moulded into an eternal creation. And know one day you'll be on the front row of Heaven's chorus, cheerleading future generations until Christ returns.[2]

Can I get a WHOOP WHOOP!

Exodus 9 v 16 *"But I have raised you up for this very purpose, that I might show you my power and that my Name may be proclaimed in all the earth."*

[1] Romans 8 v 28 / [2] Hebrews 12 v1

Drop 20 ~ Death and resurrection

I am studying at the moment and there's a module on philosophy, which in my opinion has to be the *saddest* topic in the whole world. There's this guy called Descartes who spent a large portion of his life searching for one pure thought. After much time he came up with the idea that if he was thinking he must therefore exist. Hence the phrase 'I think therefore I am'. I have been thinking about what I believe as a Christian. When everything else in life is stripped away, what is my one pure thought or thing that I can hold to? For me it has to be the divine power of the death and resurrection of Jesus.

I would much rather have said it was my relationship with God, I'm really into that, or my knowledge of God's faithfulness, that is great too…but without the death and resurrection we would have nothing. That was and is the one sure thing, the event that everything else in this world and the next hinges on! In our lives we will have "death" or difficult experiences, it is a simple fact. God gives us choices, if we choose to die to ourselves and yield to God's will we will have the resurrection, the victory, the blessing of God's loving and perfect will in our lives.

One year my kids planted sunflower seeds and they grew into these enormous beasts of plants. The head weighed as much as a small child and we had to stake them up to big wooden poles, they were so humungous. In each head of the flower were hundreds of seeds. But for those seeds to be useful the sunflower had to die first….Do you know, each little seed that came from this one flower has the capacity to multiply and reproduce, to bear fruit? Is this not what we want to do for God's kingdom?

There's a hurting world out there that needs to know Him. I want to challenge you, are you prepared to die to yourself? To embrace God's way for your life? It may mean dying to certain desires, but when we choose to do God's will over our own we have that power of the resurrection; like the sunflower the fruit that is birthed will be phenomenal, and abundant, and we will be blessed.

I think that's a pretty good foundational pure thing upon which to grow life into and out of. Where can you scatter seeds of resurrection life today?

John 12 v 24 "I tell you the truth unless a grain of wheat falls to the ground and dies, it remains a single seed. But if it dies it produces many seeds."

Drop 21 ~ Mistakes allowed!

Did you know that the person who never made a mistake, never made anything? Girlfriends we live in a world where perfection is the lie of life. No-one's boobs are that pert or skin that flawless. No one's life is that perfect and no one gets it right all the time and that's normal! In fact it's a good thing because it allows us to grow in graciousness. It's a dead cert that we will all get it wrong on occasions, because we all make mistakes.... But if we change our perspective on our mistakes we can learn to embrace the lessons they teach us. I have made many mistakes and have loads more to make I'm sure... but the ones I've learned from are where I've been loved and encouraged by others to give it another go and get back in the game. Yeah, not getting it right is embarrassing and uncomfortable but from another perspective babe...it's totally good for your humility!

I love Peter in the Bible, he's a guy who fluffs it time after time yet he was the rock upon which Jesus chose to build the church. King David in the Old Testament got blocked, had an affair and murdered rings around him but God was still able to use him. I doubt if the mistakes we might make in our world of small group relationships, church or work will ever land you in as much trouble as some of the Bible characters.

Communities grow where people feel safe to make mistakes. Sadly some groups are immature in graciousness and they get aspects of the journey wrong, which supports the perfection lie. So the circle continues! If you find you're in one of theses vicious circles don't lose heart, God will only allow this for so long before He acts and trust me He will act.... Your role is to keep praying, keep loving and developing in your relationship with God. As we grow in graciousness we melt the lie of perfection!

Are you willing to have a go and get it wrong? Honey bun, you wouldn't be cross with a toddler for falling over as they learned to walk would you? Of course not you'd help them up and encourage them to try again. This is the way God works with us when we muck it up. Let's try and see our brothers and sisters in Christ as wonderful opportunities to exercise graciousness and encouragement when they get it wrong. You see when we dare to admit to our mistakes we actually free others to admit to theirs. Girls lets get humble and stop worrying about getting it all right, there are many ways to skin a cat so dare to do it your way with all the wonderful creativity God has placed in you and have a go...

If you're the sort of person who likes all the i's dotted and t's crossed there's grace in accepting a different standard than you mike like from time to time. Do worry about not being good enough … you are more than that already! Princess…cut yourself or maybe others some slack – mistakes are allowed!

Proverbs 19 v 11 *"A man's wisdom gives him patience; it is to his glory to overlook an offence."*

Drop 22 ~ No pets allowed

I have really been thinking about this freedom thing and what this really means. God has told me that in my life there are areas I need to take responsibility for if I'm going to get the completeness that I'm after. Do you know we can keep things that oppress and burden us like unwanted pets without knowing it? We can become so accustomed to the pet of depression, or the pet of self pity wallowing in our world that we accept the lie that these things are 'just who we are'. We lose sight of the fact that these feelings, behaviours have no right to hang around our lives like stray cats. Unconsciously, we can carry them around, feel responsible for their maintenance and feed them with our anxieties. It is this rehearsing of past behaviours which keeps them alive in our today. This is actually documented by psychologists. It's why many of us are so exhausted all the time… even small luggage gets heavy if carried for a long time!

We all do this, don't we...? Lay stuff at the feet of Jesus only to pick it up again 5 mins later… Freedom is one of God's promises … and it's something worth pursuing. If there is something in your life, which has dogged you, go to God, get with Him. I believe it's God's purpose for us to live in freedom, and that experience will be as individual as we all are.

Ask God to help you, to show you if you are harbouring any unwanted pets and how you can set them down so they can walk off out of your life! Be aware though, you may be comfortable with your pet…Your pet lie, your pet anger, your pet denial may have been there a long time but unwanted pets hold you back so they gotta go, Babe! This may be a process or it may happen in an instant but I want to encourage you to at least do something about it, don't keep old pets; they become smelly and incontinent! When we're tempted to return and pick up old habits God has promised He'll make a way out of the temptation. We simply don't have to stay passively in the mire!

If spiritually you find yourself visiting the same weary places (and we all do, from time to time) go to an older Christian whom you can trust and talk it through. Allow them to stand with you before God so that His loving truth can work in you. I've been blessed in my life to have benefited from the loving and at times uncomfortable truth from a wiser person in the faith who really cares. Embrace these folks in your world they are your greatest gift and one day you may be able to return the blessing of perspective to them. If you have been carrying something heavy and cumbersome make the choice not to carry it another moment… Whatever is dogging you know that today it can get off and walk, look that sucker right in the eye and take dominion!!

Phil 4 v 13 *"I can do all things, through Christ who strengthens me"* even if that's to say 'get off and walk' to uninvited guests!

Drop 23 ~ Guilt-free zone

For God so loved the world that He gave His one and only son, that whosoever believes in Him shall not perish but have eternal life. For God did not send His son into the world to ***condemn*** the world, but to save the world through Him.[1]

I was brought up as an Irish Catholic so I reckon I can speak with some authority on the subject of guilt! *(Only joking to all the beautiful Catholics in the world, Irish or otherwise.)* Anyway I'm pretty flawed, we all are… In fact it is precisely because I'm flawed that I choose to be a follower of Jesus Christ. I know I need to go back again and again and confess my mess to the only one who can sort it. God is never surprised by what we do – He picks us up, dusts us down, teaches us and sets us back on track, again and again. How totally patient is our Lord God?

No other religion in the world offers the gift of grace as the way to life eternal!

When voices in my head accuse me about the insidious bits of sin in my life I know I have justification… You see I have a promise… No matter how bratty my attitude, how rancid my heart, how selfish my behaviour, my Jesus will never leave me nor forsake me.[2] AND… He will complete the good work He started in me and see it through to completion.[3] How cool is that? Actually that was two promises wasn't it...? Doh!

Our nature is to give up when we get it wrong and be like 'what's the point of trying' but that's exactly what the accuser wants. He wants us to give up on ourselves so he can stick the boot in while we're down! He comes at us with a big stick to clobber us. Jesus comes at us with Love: gentle, assuring, life giving, gracious, healing love!

Next time you get that sinking feeling of condemnation, stop and realise you don't need to defend yourself because you can speak the truth and confess "YES, I'm a sinner but my Jesus came and has washed me clean and I'm going to be with Him in glory regardless!" The fact of the matter is you don't need to defend yourself because Jesus has covered over your gaffs, your mess, your sin with His cleansing blood and you are redeemed forever – period! Don't get seduced in to debating the fact girlfriend that's just what your enemy wants. Stride forth in freedom from condemnation you are totally free… Now go and clobber the accuser over the head with this verse from Hosea…

Hosea 13 v 14 *"I will ransom them from the power of hell, I will redeem them from death."* Hallelujah!

The promises I mentioned above aren't just for me, they're for all of us forever! Why not look up the promises listed below… Enjoy!

[1] John 3 v 16 & 17
[2] Hebrews 13 v 5
[3] Philippians 1 v 6

Drop 24 ~ God the master surgeon

I once watched a programme about a man called John Merrick, also known as the elephant man. It is a terribly, terribly sad and beautiful story. This man suffered from a disease, which in childhood had horribly mutated his body especially his head and face. He was rejected by His family and thrown out to live on the streets. For much of his life he was laughed at and scorned because of his deformity.

He could do nothing about his imperfections, other than cover himself with a mask and trade his appearance in freak shows… One day he met a man who was to change his life. That man was Dr. Fredrick Treves a skilled surgeon who befriended him. He took care of the elephant man's physical needs. He was kind to him. He talked with him, got to know him and discovered the person who was on the inside…truly a humbling story.

I found myself thinking through the whole film that before God I'm a bit like John Merrick myself. Ponder that for a moment… Before the Almighty God…in comparison to the angels' norm that is beauty of heaven, what do we look like?

Just like the elephant man we are all imperfect, even grotesque, before God's Throne… and just like the elephant man there is nothing we can do about our imperfections. It's why God, the almighty creator, healer, restorer stepped into time two thousand years ago. He left us a master surgeon, the Holy Spirit…who works with us, who loves us just as we are…UGLY…

Just like the elephant man, we have been befriended by the friend above all friends[1] who has the power to transform us. Through layer upon layer the loving surgeon works on us from the inside out. Little by little He transforms our inner person into something beautiful if we let him.[2] There will be times the surgery will hurt and we will have to be totally still when enduring the surgeon's knife, trusting in His expertise. Our master surgeon may need to do reconstructive work a number of times in the same area of the most deformed or damaged bits of who you are. Recovery may be slower than you'd like or scar tissue may take a while to bond.

But dearly beloved child of God know this: He never puts any one of His children through pain lightly and if there would be another way He'd do it. As you wince His heart anguishes, but He loves you too much to leave you as you are. As you surrender to His will over yours in life, accepting the different techniques of surgery and humbling yourself to trust your most vulnerable wounds to His hands, you can be assured He knows what He's doing.[3]

My heart is breaking for some of you and what is exploding in your world as I write this. The falleness of this world at times does indeed suck. But if you want to get mad, get mad at the one who causes the destruction not the creator who catches your every tear, who cherishes your every whisper... allow yourself to be wrapped up in His comforting embrace.[4]

If you feel like the pain of surgery is too much at times it's totally ok to cry out to Him. The Bible has an anaesthetic just for you. 'Be still and know that I am the Lord.'[5] His promise to you is that He will work ALL THINGS for your good according to His good plan and purpose.[6]

You are beautiful but not as beautiful as you're going to be…

Lamentations 3 v 32 - 33 *"Though He brings grief, He will show compassion, so great is His unfailing love; for He does not willingly bring affliction of grief to the children of men."*

Look up the following verses and highlight them in your Bible, you'll be surprised one day when you're flicking through how they speak to you.

[1] Proverbs 18 v 24
[2] Philippians 3 v 21
[3] Job 38 v 36-37
[4] Isaiah 66 v 13
[5] Psalm 46 v 10
[6] Romans 8 v 28

Drop 25 ~ Step right up

Hebrews 10 v 19 – 22 says, *"So friends, we can now, without hesitation, walk right up to God into 'The Holy Place'. Jesus has cleared the way by the blood of His sacrifice, acting as our priest before God. The 'curtain' into God's presence is His body. So let's do it – full of confidence that we are presentable inside and out. Let's keep a grip on His promises which keep us going."* (Message Bible)

Have you ever found yourself wanting to blend into the wall paper because you feel like you're not at the same level of wonderfulness as the company you find yourself in? I have! I remember we had these rich rellies who for some reason always made me feel inferior. Perhaps it's because my mother would spend hours cleaning our home before they arrived (our house was much smaller than theirs) or the sense of tension as we all had to present ourselves with clean hands and faces to my mother. What is that all about…? The rest of your body can be scanky but as long as your hands and face are clean, it's grand? Anyway…

I've been at big churchy events where I felt all the movers and shakers were so oozing joy-filled super glow; I just couldn't compete not even if I pretended and tried to be as spiritual as them! Gosh now I think of it why am I even writing this book! Nah, reject that…and get back to the point. Ok, which was feeling like you don't quite measure up.

Often I've felt like on the outside I can fake it, I can even talk a credible talk, but if people knew how I yelled at the kids or thought angry thoughts about people they'd shun me quicker than they could sneeze. However that's exactly it…followers of Christ need to be real about who we are to each other. The world is so full of wounded people faking their way through life that it's hard to know who's real or part plastic. Sadly some Christians have fallen into this trap too. They feel or even act superior because they 'know' some secret that God can only reveal to them 'cause they're so gifted in the prophetic or some other such thing. (I'm not knocking prophecy it's truly a wonderful gift when used for the glory of God's agenda and not man's.) Here's the thing; fake-ness looks like what it is when considered closely. It's good to remember we're all as equally awful and yet through Christ wonderful at the same time!

We all don't measure up to the ideal but because and only because of what Jesus has done we can confidently feel like we belong in the most holy of places. Just stop and think about that for a mo'… Right now you can walk straight in to the throne room of God, not feel intimidated because you're not as good as …. You can simply enter in and know to your Friend and King you are acceptably presentable. Who you are is good enough!

"If you are truly humble nothing can touch you, not humiliation or praise because you will know who you are." Mother Teresa

Don't fake it babe, who you are is good enough!

Drop 26 ~ It's your move

We must make the first move!! In Revelation it says, "Behold I stand at the door and knock." I love that God never forces himself upon us. He waits to be invited. It's up to us; we must choose to open the door and go through or stand outside. In life so often we hold back from taking the plunge and opening the door. We hold back from entering in to any relationships which go deeper than the superficial because we fear being hurt and people do at times hurt very much. We hold back because we hate causing offence and we abhor being vulnerable.

If you're breathing you'll have experienced the pain of rejection. Perhaps it was the cool girls at school or the skinny yummy Mummies at the school gate, wherever and whenever we've all been there. It hurts when we feel like we're on the outside looking in. Girlfriend Jesus knew what it felt like to be an outsider, it is why His church is 'all inclusive'. He wants you to know the comfort and security of belonging. He wants you to enter into a union with Him where you'll be known by the one who created you. But He also wants you to relate to His body here on earth and I guess at times that's the scary bit.

His BIG idea is the church…it's a collection of flawed individuals, you and me regardless of denomination. So if it's really important to God I figure it should be important to us too. We need to see that each person in our world is no accident. They are a divine opportunity to demonstrate God's love. They are a divine opportunity to invest in eternity through our interactions with them. It may be just a smile or a comment, on the other hand it may be what you don't say when you could! 'Whatever you do, do it all for the glory of God.'[1]

God needs <u>you</u> today to pick up the phone, send a card, say a prayer, smile a smile, just reach out and connect. It may not be as cosy and safe as nodding at someone from the other side of your office. But it's your move and God has prepared conversations, acts of kindness and much more for you to do in advance.[2] You don't have to be everyone's new best friend but you can take a step deeper and get to know and therefore love on a deeper level.

You go girl…! The world needs you…

2 Timothy 1 v 7 *"For you did not give us a spirit of timidity, but a Spirit of power, of love and a sound mind"*

[1] 2 Cor 10 v 31 / [2] Ephesians 4 v 12 -13

Drop 27 ~ Knowledge is power

When a person has knowledge on a subject they quite simply have the advantage should that knowledge ever be needed. So for example my motor mechanic has the advantage of knowing about car engines where I don't so he has the power to deceive me or not. They could tell me anything and I'd be powerless to question him/her as I don't know a thing about engines! In a way I would be at their mercy because of my ignorance. I'm not a high brow academic (*as you can tell from reading so far!)* but that doesn't excuse me not making the best of what I've got. It's up to me to clue myself into car maintenance or bus timetables or whatever else I need to navigate this life. Our Christian walk is no different babe….

When we don't know God (and the best way to know Him is by reading His book) we are vulnerable to all the unscrupulous powers and principalities which fly around looking for opportunities to exploit God's children.[1] When we know God through His word, we are empowered and can be proactive in our own protection. Did you know when we live lives submitted to God, we can resist the devil and He will have to flee from us? When tempted we can declare 1 Cor 10 v13 *'there is no temptation that's new and God will make a way out for you if you're sincere in wanting a way out' (paraphrased).* When feeling shaken and doubtful with God, we can declare Romans 8 v 17 'I am a child of God' and John 10 v 28 'No one can snatch me out of my Father's hand'. When we're struggling with frustrations declare, "Sod off Satan…" Oh no, that's not in the Bible but it's ok to say it anyway…

Sweet cheeks, the more you know the truth, the more power you have when you need it and precious sister you *will* need it! Join a Bible study group or start one and learn together; take a book of the Bible and read a chapter a day, look up the Bible references at the bottom of each page in this book, take note of where a sermon has been preached from then go back and re-read it for yourself. Only Open The Book! Don't allow yourself to be ignorant, for a time will come when your friends will ask you why you believe what you believe about God and you're going to need answers. So gen up now…in doing so you'll build yourself up and be strong in God.

In today's multi-media market place there are sermons to download, channels to watch and wise people to talk to. In short there's no excuse for not gaining knowledge about the things of God. There are some great books out there to help you find a place to start, but knowledge is power and you, princess of the kingdom of heaven, need to hone and develop what God has given you! It says in Isaiah…

Isaiah 11 v 2 *"The Spirit of the Lord will rest upon him, the spirit of wisdom and understanding, the Spirit of counsel and of power, the Spirit of knowledge and of the fear of the Lord – and he will delight in the fear of the Lord. He will not judge by what he sees with his eyes or decides by what he hears with his ears; but with righteousness..."*

[1] 1 Peter 5 v 8

Drop 28 ~ Feeding your fruit trees

John 15 describes how we are to be like vine branches, feeding from the main tree. The only real fruit we can produce is the fruit of what we're rooted in. A man called Barney Coombs used to say, 'What's hidden in the roots is revealed in the shoots.' I am passionate about the fruit I produce in my life. I want it to taste sweet, be appealing and fragrant. I want it to please the head gardener. So how do I help myself to grow in the garden of God? I want my fruit to be of value and worth and totally desirable to the world. What we dig into the soil of our soul will show in how we outwork this thing called salvation....

Proverbs 7 v 17 & 19 says, *"I love those who love me, and those who seek me find me. v 19 - My fruit is better than fine gold; what I yield surpasses choice silver."* So I reckon that obeying the teachings of Christ, modelling our lives on godly men and women, and sowing seeds of wisdom into our daily lives is a good place to start the fertilization of our souls. I have written out some words of wisdom from people I see as wise and stuck them in my study. Here are some of my favourites. I hope they bring life to you and feed your soul.

"The way I experience God's presence is unique to me." (John Ortberg)[1]

"If you don't submit your vision to God, your vision may become your god" (Alan Molineux)

"The tragedy of life is what dies inside a man while he lives." (Albert Einstein)

"Peace is not the absence of trouble rather the presence of God." (Anon)

"Anybody can be great, because everybody can serve. You don't need any special skills, just a heart full of grace and a soul generated by love." (Martin Luther King)

"Loneliness is not the absence of faces it's the absence of intimacy. Loneliness doesn't come from being alone: it comes from feeling alone." (Max Lucado)[2]

"He who is good at making excuses is seldom good for anything else" (Benjamin Franklin)

and finally.....

"If you don't succeed at first then try and try again." (Wright Brothers)

Jeremiah 17 v 7-8 *"But blessed is the man who trusts in the Lord, whose confidence is in Him. He will be like a tree planted by streams of water, that sends out roots by the stream. It does not fear when heat comes; its leaves are always green. It has no worries in a year of drought and never fails to bear fruit."*

Why don't you find a few of your own and stick them on your fridge to encourage you?

[1]John Ortberg, *'God is Closer Than you Think'* p. 25, 2005 :Zondervan Press
[2]Max Lucado, *'Travelling Light'* p.109, 2001 :Warner Publishing Group USA

Drop 29 ~ How's your smell?

"When you enter a room enhance it with the aroma of Christ."[1]

When I was a child my Mum used to say that our mood or attitude was like a smell, in that you could be a pleasant aroma and nice to be around, or you could stink to high Heaven and be worth avoiding. There are times when we all stink from the inside out and I was thinking about this... I wondered, can we help ourselves to be less offensive? Yes I know there are some folks who enjoy the smell or their own wind which is kinda just weird! But most of us want to be fragrant from the inside out don't we?

Like all bodies, we've all got our smelly bits! Let's be honest here, this is normal…Perhaps your smelly issue is hurt pride or a past misunderstanding. It might be resentment where you yearn to *get even* with your nemesis. Babe, whatever the issue being harboured, be aware it really does make for a nasty smell in the fragrance of who you are. Just like we wash regularly and spritz our underarms, I believe we can choose to put on the aroma of Christ. We can choose to give our pride to God and be of no reputation in the eyes of our peers. We can choose to be humble when confronted with our own humanity. We can choose to speak words which will bring healing and reconciliation into a situation. We can choose to forgive and leave justice with God as we're commanded to do!

What's scary about holding on to the crap of life is that after a time you become acclimatised to the smell and while everyone else smells you, you can't smell yourself! I have people in my world who'll tell me out of genuine love for me that my breath smells or my attitude sucks. I praise God for them, they are a joy to me…ok maybe not all the time… but I have come to value these mirrors in my world.

One of my favourite stories in the Bible is found in John 12 where Mary humbles herself to wash the feet of Jesus and pours expensive perfume over Him. She chooses to leave her past behind, act with abandoned humility and great cost …the result? The whole room was filled with fragrance and Jesus was honoured. Girl don't you want to be a bit like that? I want to enhance the peace of the world I inhabit with the aroma of Christ don't you? We can learn a lot from how Mary acted that night…

Thought food: is there something smelly from the past you need to wash off? Take some time to meditate and pray that through, ask the Holy Spirit to reveal what

He wants to…then liberally spray on the fragrance of the aroma of Christ. Ephesians 5 v 1 – *"Be imitators of God, live as dearly loved children and live a life of love, just as Christ loved us and gave himself up for us as a fragrant offering and sacrifice to God."*

[1]2 Corinthians 2 v 14

Drop 30 ~ Pull it apart and ask why

I read this quote somewhere by someone I can't remember… "Take your mind out every now and then and dance on it. If you don't it will get all caked up." I love the challenge in that… I wish I knew who wrote it, doh! Often the pride of our own opinion and the need to be right puts up a wall to listening. When we're confronted with something different or challenging to our own beliefs we can get total brain freeze and our minds shut down, rendering us blinkered.

When I first met my husband I used to joke with him saying 'What's our opinion on this?' *(because he's dead clever)!* If I'm honest I know now I wanted him to save me the effort of pulling a subject apart, of examining it and having to take the responsibility for my own conclusions. It's interesting because this is the crux of our relationship with God. He wants us to pull things apart and ask "Why?" I believe He wants us to THINK for ourselves, to look at different perspectives and know why we believe what we believe. It is our responsibility to find out why we hold the views we do. When we die and go to Heaven, God will hold us to account for our life choices, borne out of our beliefs. He won't be interested in the most popular Christian philosophies; He'll be interested in yours! Ouch babe, I hope this isn't too challenging?

God wants each of us, in step with His Holy Spirit, to be the catalyst for our own development. So if for example you think women shouldn't be in leadership ask yourself why? What does His word say and don't just look in the NIV! Read up, talk to wise people, examine all the evidence, seek the truth and you will find it.[1] Be encouraged nothing that you'll research will ever be wasted. Don't sit passively and accept the group legalism, the Pharisees did that and they were the most repressed unhappy bunch on the face of the earth!

It's so easy to take something as fact when more often than not it's only a part of the story. Sometimes if we knew just one more piece of information we'd totally change our view point. When we are actively pulling issues apart and asking questions about them we are working out your salvation with serious sincerity. I think that Glorifies God! Take your mind out it's a beautiful thing knead it, dance with it, even stomp on it if you have to but use it girlfriend! It's a wonderful thing…. I love the quote on the next page – enjoy!

Philippians 2 v 12 *"Therefore my dear friends – continue to work out your salvation with fear and trembling, for it is God who works in you to will and act according to His good purpose."*

Quote: "If in the last few years you haven't discarded a major opinion or acquired a new one, check your pulse. You may be dead." (Gelett Burgess)

[1]Luke 11 v 9-10

Drop 31 ~ Iddy biddy things

When I was a child people used the expression: "Take care of the pennies and the pounds will take care of themselves." When we take care of the little things in our world the big things are often kept from becoming big things. As followers of Christ we can be really blessed because God sees the small things and honours them. He sees when we refuse to take part in gossip and it blesses His heart. He understands when we resist from giving a piece of our mind to the person that's got on our last nerve. He sees the pain of staying put when you want to walk away. He cherishes the small things you do babe. He notices.

One of my favourite Bible teachers Dr.Tayo Adeyemi says: "Pay attention to the little things, because great doors swing on little hinges." Isn't that so true? When we let our standards slip our character is eroded little by little. The flames of love in our hearts grow cooler and we start to sleep walk in the things of God rather than run the race with passion.[1] I know when I miss my prayer times with God I am depleted in wisdom and strength and if you've read thus far you'll know how much I really need His wisdom! I've found that I need to be filled with God more than daily! If you're like me it's more of a moment by moment thing as I wrestle with the frustrations of the 'little things'.

How are the little things in your world today? Are you keeping your relationship passionate by praise, prayer and drinking in the presence of Jesus? When did you last set aside time just to sit still before your King and be filled with peace, joy, love, kindness, patience and self control?[2]
It is so crucial to do an internal audit of the little things from time to time...

In America there's a website which encourages it's readers to invest in the little things in other people through random acts of kindness. It's not Christian but I got a kick out of some of the ideas...they suggest things like paying for a stranger's meal in a restaurant, leaving change in a laundry matt or giving up your seat on a bus. I so love that!!

When we live to try and think of others' needs we are investing in the servant heart we're supposed to have as followers of Christ. Why not invest spiritually this week in time with God and respond to what He places on your heart? Then just watch as God encourages you and honours the iddy biddy things you do in each moment of each day to bring Him glory. He always amazes and surprises in the iddy biddy areas of life…Be expectant!

[1]Hebrews 12 v 1-3 2.
[2]Dr. Tayo Adeyemi, New Wine Church, Woolwich London 2005
[3]Galatians 5 v22-25

Drop 32 ~ Live to please the one worth pleasing

God never said we'd be in the lead at half time, only that we'd win the game!!

I have a chronic condition known as foot in mouth. When I meet someone I admire I have this amazing ability of saying something totally inappropriate or I just dry up altogether. So often I wish I could go back and phrase the thing I just said differently or speak up instead of whimping out. Are you feeling any of this? When God gives me a weird instruction that makes no sense to me, do I risk my pride and possibly the recipient's sanity and get on with delivering that word? I have to admit there have been many times when I have been too cowardly to exercise the prophetic gifting God has given me for fear of causing offence. And yet the Bible tells me that I should live to please God rather than man.[1] I'll tell you something else, I've always regretted not following the Holy Spirit's prompting and have often seen God use another person to do what He called me to do!

Imagine if Hudson Taylor had decided never to go back to China after he lost His first wife and his first child to typhoid and had nothing but faith to pay for his trip. Or consider… if Mother Teresa had preferred cleanliness and nice smells rather than the squalor of the gutters, or sought a position in the Vatican rather than the streets of Calcutta.

These remarkable people never knew at the time they were writing history, in fact a lot of the time they were on their knees in despair thinking they'd totally blown it. I really believe great giants in the faith wrestled just as we do, to wonder if they had even left the starting blocks never mind the joy of a rest at half time. Princess, in the 'day to day'-ness of life we can forget that when we're living to please God and walking in obedience to Him, He can use our clumsy efforts we make to shape His purposes here on earth.

We sing a kid's song at our church and a line from it goes, 'how wonderful to be a part of God's amazing plan…' and that's just it folks it is amazing, what a risk taker is our God, eh? Would I choose me? Nah… but God did! And what's more He promises to equip me for what He's called me to do….Yippee![2] We will win the game, of that we are assured…. we just don't know how yet!

Next time you think you've messed up, or fear or discouragement overtakes you remember it's not how it looks from this side of eternity!!
May I Pray this prayer with you…?

Hebrews 13 v 20…

May the God of peace, who through the blood of the eternal covenant brought back from the dead our Lord Jesus that great Shepherd of sheep, equip you with everything good for doing his will and may He work in us, what is pleasing to Him, through Jesus Christ to whom be glory for ever and ever…Amen.

[1]Ephesians 5 v 8-9 [2]2 Timothy 3 v16-17

Drop 33~ Ouch even nice people can hurt…!

I know some of the most beautiful people in terms of whom they are on the inside, but even really lovely people stuff up occasionally. You see sweet cheeks just because you're a Christian trying hard to please the Lord doesn't mean you're not going to get up someone else's nose from time to time...! And vice versa... But Hunny bun, how we react to the niggles of relationship can bring forth life by exposing the areas in *us* which need addressing. Perhaps those people in our lives who rub us up the wrong way are our greatest blessing in disguise because they are God's tool for sanding down those calloused areas of the soul. Isn't it often aspects of your own character flaws which you see in others that annoy you the most!

Mmmm… Just stop for a moment and think about that for a moment. How do you react when someone says something really tactless or even down right rude? What pushes your buttons for me it's injustice, or disloyalty, *in fact now I'm thinking about it….* Ok best not think for too long on that one!! Anyho…ask yourself are you Ms Angry Pants when offended or are you attentive to what the Holy Spirit is showing you about yourself. Can you step back from the situation and bathe that annoying person in Agape and pray for grace to act for God's glory? Ouch, I know easily said, and putting it in action is another level!

Babe you can do it with God's help![1] Precious sister, our wonderful God wants you to be free from all the prickly, niggley, yuck that holds you back from abundance of life…His antidote is Himself - love, but to be given love you need to humble your heart, unclench your fists and receive. This requires vulnerability; when our arms are wide open we can feel wide open to love or hate. It goes against our human instinct to allow ourselves to be vulnerable but when we proactively trust in God's protection every aspect of our defence is covered. While we need use our God-given discernment in whom we allow near the areas of our heart marked 'fragile' we can trust God totally and allow Him access to all areas.

Precious child… God will never harm you or hate you.[2] He hates your sin but you child …He loves you with an everlasting love. God sent his son to die for you when you were at your most vile… while you spat, scratched and hissed at Him, He opened His arms wide to you. He didn't care about the pain, He simply cared for you. We will probably never be as vulnerable as Christ was on that cross exhausted, naked and bleeding. To open up to God is the safest thing you'll ever do again and again.

Going to your intimate place with God one on one, pouring your heart out to Him is the safest place you'll ever know this side of heaven.

Precious sister- you are no accident, God has placed you in the world for this time, this day, this NOW. Don't allow misunderstandings and hurts to imprison you. Christ needs you! You are part of His plan, we need you, I need you, please, please, please, next time you feel like withdrawing because you've been hurt, hang on in there, examine whatever happened in your safe place with God, learn from it and grow; but whatever you do stay in the game.

Philippians 3 v 14 "*I press on towards the goal to win the prize for which God has called me heavenward in Christ.*"

1. Phil 4 v13 Strength
2. Deut 33 v 27 Everlasting Love

Drop 34 ~ Who will you pass the baton on to?

There's a Chinese proverb which says, "If you want one year of prosperity, grow grain. If you want ten years of prosperity, grow trees. If you want one hundred years of prosperity – grow people." I'm so glad I married into all that oriental wisdom! Let me ask you a question, who are you a role model for? You might think who me, no one…! But look closer. Do you have younger women in your world? Nieces, friends' girls, daughters; if you have then, Sweetie pie, you are a role model whether you like it or not.

I thought (when I was growing up) that Christian women had to wear special *ugly* make up, have a biblical opinion-bypass operation, a humour lobotomy and hairy legs. Not to mention implants to help them get really excited about flower arranging, brownies and little kittens, argh…! Kill me now!! Is it any wonder from an early age the thought of morphing into this awful person filled me with horror…!

Thankfully God wants me to be me… I know people who'd love me not to be me… but that's another story! God has made you uniquely you for a reason. He needs you to stand up and walk tall in the uniqueness of who you are. Princess, God invented cutting edge… so don't try and be who you are not. Just as you are is all you need to be. You can be on trend, womanly, sassy, have an opinion and even wear nail varnish….Oooh…! By being you in a Godly way you will be a role model for the next generation and not put them off… Who said Christians had to be bland anyway? You may be a tobacco chewing, sock it to 'em fire-filled woman of strength; you may be a quite gentle sensitive flower or all of the above, only **be yourself** to all the fullness of Christ in you! Have a wee think…who is in your world that you can invest time, encouragement and love into? Are there jobs within your church you could do to 'grow' the next generation? Are there opportunities you could construct to give others a leg up?

It takes humility not to seek reward for yourself, but to invest in the dreams of others. The deal is… if you want to find favour in God's eyes He esteems the humble in heart. Girls, we've got to work at building a community and culture within the church which cuts the ground and makes a pathway for those coming up behind. When we dare to be ourselves and to build up those coming behind selflessly, the world will see and authenticity shines bright. Trust me, you may not be aware of it but someone will notice this week how you speak, how you build up or tear down, if you look like a frump or a force to be reckoned with….it's good to be aware it's not only Christ who's watching you.[1]

Proverbs 5 v 21 *"For a man's/ woman's ways are in full view of the Lord and he examines all his paths."*

Drop 35 ~ Paraphrase your own bit

One of the best ways as a starting point of getting to grips with the Bible is to take a passage and paraphrase it. That just means write what you understand from it in your own words. That's what I want you to do today – Day 35! Take your favourite Psalm or section, write it in your own words and pray that the Holy Spirit will inspire you. Here's mine…

Hebrews 12 v 1-6 "Therefore, since we are surrounded by such a great cloud of witnesses, let us throw off everything that hinders and the sin that so easily entangles, and let us run with perseverance the race marked out for us. Let us fix our eyes on Jesus the author and perfecter of our faith, who for the joy set before Him endured the cross scorning it's shame, and sat down at the right hand of the throne of God. Consider Him who endured such opposition from sinful men, so that you do not grow weary and lose heart. In your struggle against sin you have not yet resisted to the point of shedding your blood. And you have forgotten that word of encouragement that addresses you as sons."

Paraphrased... *So since we have such supportive friends, who'll help us when the going gets tough, let's get rid of all the rubbish in our lives, and choose to go for it and let nothing hold us back from our personal walk with God. Look at Jesus, He's the guy who's written and knows the whole story of our lives from beginning to end. He humbled himself to die horribly for you, because He knew the big picture. Think about what He went through because He loved you and be encouraged. We will have difficult things to walk through in this life and they are different for each person. But don't give up; all things happen for a reason, God is in control and loves you even when a situation might make you question that love. When things are really hard pray, press into him, talk to Him, as a youngster would to a Father who is nuts about His child.*

Ok now it's your turn, baby cakes: go open up the Bible and get paraphrasing and have fun… When you've done that, stick it up in the loo or on the fridge (somewhere you'll see it) and be encouraged. Suggestions… should you get stuck!

Isaiah 61 v 1- 3
Lamentations 3 v 22 – 26
Psalm 139 v 1-14
2 Corinthians 1 v 3 -7

Drop 36 ~ Microwave mentality anybody?

We live in a consumer hurry up, have it now, pay later culture. We have instant chips, instant makeovers, instant banking…there's so much we can get at the touch of a button on our computer screen, except things delivered on time but that's Great Britain! I often hear people saying that life is so busy and rushed, and yet we have so many labour saving devices. So why is life so hectic? In many of our churches holiness seems to be kind of linked to how busy you are with 'the Lord's work'. Do you know what… people are the 'Lord's work'!! If in the business of life we have lost our grip on God's priorities, we're too busy! If rotas and budgets and general paper pushing comes before people we're too busy. No one on their death bed said I wish I'd spent more time at work!

I have had the privilege of meeting many wonderful Christians who are inspirations to me. The ones who stand the test of time are the ones who have learned to resist the temptation to microwave their lives. Jesus never rushed, oh he was purposed and holy but he never rushed! Look at the story of the sick girl in Mathew 9 or Lazarus in John 11. Jesus spent so much time with his Father he was totally in step with His leading through the Holy Spirit. A good wine can't be rushed to maturity and neither can you. It takes time for wisdom to develop and the Holy Spirit being part of the Godhead will be rushed no more than Jesus. If Jesus never rushed then why do we?

It takes time for a tree to put roots down into the soil and draw up the nutrients it needs to grow. In the same way it takes time for you through feeding on the word of God and putting it into practice in your life to develop spiritual growth. Staying with the tree analogy, let's pretend you're a fruit tree… a big juicy succulent fruit tree. Heaven's fruit, 'the fruit of the spirit is love, joy, peace, patience, kindness, goodness, faithfulness, gentleness and self–control'.[1] To grow this fruit takes nurturing and requires regular care. If you want your *joy berry, your love berry, etc.* to grow, work at being joyful especially when you least feel like it!

Jesus isn't micro waving the wedding feast of His bride (the church). No, he is painstakingly, with great care and detail, making preparations for the meal of a lifetime.[2] He is organising and prioritising for the appointed time when the Godhead will wrap things up, the trumpet will sound and the last day will come and Heaven will be our home!

Psalm 130 *"I wait for the Lord, my soul waits, and in His word I put my hope. My soul waits for the Lord more than watchmen wait for the morning (say it again sister) more than watchmen wait for the morning."*

[1]Galatians 5 v 22
[2]Rev 19 v 9

Drop 37 ~ <u>If Only…</u>

How often do you hear people say, if only? We spend a lot of time looking in life for something which will satisfy. Our Western culture is geared to keeping us slightly dissatisfied. While one half of the world wants food and shelter we want… well… we just want more!!! If only I had more money, if only I was married to that person, if only I lived in this house or had those things I'd be happy… **guys we need to open our eyes and see 'if only' is a lie of Satan, don't swallow it!**

The reality of life is imperfection, but when we choose to focus on what we have rather than what we *think* we want, we can get free of the 'if only' mind trap. God knows what we need; heck He even wants us to live in a way which makes us feel blessed. When we focus on completing ourselves through things rather than Him we leave a welcome mat of dissatisfaction for our enemy.

When you seek first the kingdom of God you have access to peace that surpasses all understanding. Jesus is the only thing that will ever truly satisfy. He is the person who knows you better than you know yourself. He knows what you need; He knows what will bless you and bring you abundance of life. If you have Godly goals for your life, brilliant… surrender those to Him, do what you need to practically, then get on with enjoying what you've got!

A 'dissatisfied soul' is simply a soul which lacks appreciation for the graciousness you're living under. Start talking out loud about the blessings in your life. Hey, why not start talking and walking in faith about some of those things you want to see fulfilled. If you want a better marriage confess 'my husband is the man the Lord has joined me with and He will help me work this marriage through to His glory' or finances: 'My God is able to do more than I could ask or imagine, and will provide for all my needs.' Honey Bun, don't rob yourself of the blessings of each day by living with an 'if only' attitude. Make the best of **this day,** it might be your last!

Make time today to pray about the 'if only's' on your heart and sort out with God the difference between what you want and what He wants for you. Ask Him to forgive all the things which get taken for granted in your life and to renew a fresh ability to see all the great things you have.

1 Thessalonians 5 v 16 -18 *"Be joyful always; pray continually; give thanks in all circumstances for this is God's will for you in Christ Jesus."*

Footnote: There's no point claiming the promises of Christ if you are walking in disobedience. The biblical principle is if we want to see breakthrough we need to live in righteousness! God will answer your prayers but maybe not in your time frame or the way you think.

Drop 38 ~ I'm a fish, keep on swimming

In the film 'Finding Nemo' there's a fish called Dorry who is very absent minded. To help herself keep focused she repeats to herself: 'I'm a fish, swim, swim, swim, keep on swimming, I'm a fish …' It's hard to focus sometimes isn't it?

In the book of Exodus we can read time and time again how the Israelite people lost their direction and needed guidance. When they came to Moses and said, "What shall we do?" his response was an amazingly humble one for such a great leader. He said "I don't know, BUT……We have a God who does and in the time of uncertainty we must humble ourselves and fix our eyes on Him and in faith trust Him to bring us through."

In many churches the buzz word is Vision; in fact it's so much of a buzz word that it's often said with an Australian accent!* Sometimes in His wisdom the Lord does not afford us the luxury of vision. There are times we may not have been able to see clearly the way forward through a particular storm but have held our course, kept on swimming and come through the other side stronger in the knowledge of Christ.

We can make a place of uncertainty a place of peace when we trust in the one who knows every outcome… One thing I've learned in these blind spots is the ONLY way through is by swimming as Jesus modelled - God's way. We can blame circumstances for swimming up stream and behaving in ungodly ways. It's when we just faithfully keep swimming to the best of our ability to bring God glory that we are tested and victories are won. God is not interested in why we choose to implement what we thought was a good idea if it goes against His word; He is interested in our obedience no matter what… *(see the story of Abraham and Isaac in Genesis 22)*

It's tempting to hurry out a plan of action, or a 'new vision' when faced with uncertain or difficult situations. I have seen people lose their focus and get sidetracked from their destiny because they followed what seemed like a good idea at the time. God needs us to be alert and focused on His plan, His way in His time. Next time you are in a place like Moses and simply unsure of which direction to go let's choose to model his humility and get on our face before God. Let's choose to pray and stay there till we are saturated with His peace. Trust me, He hears your prayers.

It's tough when we are in a place like Moses was but you can be in that place *with God.* Tell yourself the truth, I'm a child of the King and I just need to keep on walking in His way, His truth and He'll give me His life… Or as 'Dorry' advises… just keep swimming!!

Romans 5 v 3 – 5 *"Let us rejoice in our suffering because we know that suffering produces perseverance, perseverance character and character hope and hope does not disappoint us because God has poured out His love into our hearts by the power of His Holy Spirit who He has given us."*

* (sorry to the Aussies reading this, I love how you talk and hope you are flattered that people have hijacked your beautiful accent)

Drop 39 ~ Interrupting heaven

Revelation 8 v 1, 3 & 4

"When he opened the 7th seal, there was silence in heaven for about half an hour... Another angel, who had a golden censer, came and stood at the altar. He was given much incense to offer, with the prayers of the saints, on the golden altar before the throne. The smoke of the incense, together with the prayers of the saints, went up before God from the angel's hand."

HOLD THE PHONE....OUR PRAYERS INTERRUPT THE WORSHIP IN HEAVEN!

Can you believe that? Our Father is like shh! Listen, one of my precious children is talking to me!! How totally humbling is that thought? Just think, the creator of the universe listens that intently to your prayers. Did you know prayerlessness is a sin?[1] I didn't for a long time. I knew it was a good thing to do but I never realised not praying was actually a sin![1] We actually carry responsibilities for prayer when we are Christians. Do you pray for your family and friends, do you pray for those who get up your nose? Do you pray about the Goliath needs of the world such as drug addiction, child prostitution or war? If not, why not? These issues are breaking God's heart.

Girls, God, for reasons we may never understand this side of Heaven, asks us to pray. Yes, He wants us to share our most intimate whispers, but He longs for us to step up and intercede for this world. We are involved in our space in time, in eternal matters of heaven.[2] Big things happen when we pray, lives are changed, the impossible is made possible, we tap into the supernatural!!

Have you ever noticed when you try to make time to pray, however, something always comes up? Our enemy will do all he can to thwart out attempts to pray. If it's not the phone ringing or the postman calling, it'll be a sudden feeling of exhaustion when you sit down to make a start. Satan wants us to stay in the sleepiness of eeny meeny mynee mo prayers; you know the ones, where you cover the bases for a few minutes and rush off towards the day. Don't settle for that... Your prayers can effect change outside time, culture or limits in the spiritual realm when you pray in the name of Jesus Christ.

Using scripture as a sword in your hand makes powers and principalities look on in terror. Girlfriend, you have the capacity in Jesus to storm the gates of hell and take back plunder and then some. Get mad about social injustice, act and pray. Get motivated by the threat of hell over your family, act and pray. Get passionate about refusing to give up on that teenager, act and pray. Don't buy the lie that there's nothing you can do… You've got the power!

One day you may be very glad God puts one of your situations on someone's heart for His divine attention in prayer.

Here are some really practical tools for helping you to pray; you don't have to do them all in one go but some may help...

- Be practical – you need head space so while cooking tea may not be the best time; while the kids watch TV in another room or you commute, choose your moment and go for it!
- Have a notepad beside you so when you remember where you left your purse or that appointment, whatever, you can write it down. (God is ok with our scattery thinking; hey we're women, we juggle!)
- Ask the Holy Spirit to help you.
- Personalise scriptures – write them out and say them till they become your own. (*Here's one of my fave's Psalm 37 v 5-6*)
- Write out the days of the week…allocate a person to a day, e.g. Mum on Monday, Children on Tuesday…
- Watch the news – it's what's happening in your nation so it's your responsibility to pray about it (even covering one news item a day in prayer is a super start).
- Pray with other people – get two friends, set aside an hour a week/ month /whatever. Take 15 mins to discuss prayer topics then get to it and pray, you'll be amazed at what you get through.

Most of all know that you WILL be distracted; recognise this then press through. Gosh as I type this I'm excited by the change to our world I know we are going to effect because of our prayers. Let's take action in the mighty name of Jesus Christ.

We've got POWER!

[1]Ephesians 6 v 18
[2]Jeremiah 29 v 12

Drop 40 ~ Your preciousness is...

Proverbs tells us to guard our heart[1]...and Matthew tells us not to give away preciousness to pigs.[2] When you wear your heart on your sleeve it is likely to get bumped! Some of us are simply open books, whatever is going on in our world will show on our faces! When I was younger I felt I owed people an explanation for everything... that, coupled with an unhealthy need to be liked exposed me to unwise disclosure which caught me out a few times. Wisdom dictates we should be careful ***who*** we open up to and tell the intimate details of our lives. It is wise to have levels of friendship; many people may know you but only those who have proved their loyalty and love towards you should have access to some of the detail... People do not have the *right* to know the small print of who you are. Did you know that?

Trust is something which takes time to build up and for good reason. God wants us to exercise wisdom and sobriety when sharing aspects of what He has so preciously placed within us. In this life's journey we will have travelling companions. Some are with you on the zippidee do dah days only and others are with you through the darkest storms. Some will build you up, and love you enough to challenge you when you go off course. These companions are in truth a gift to you. Some will indulge your whims, tell you what you want to hear and run away when the going gets rough. Learn to know which is which and love them just the same.

I see people all the time who trust with abandonment and give their heart, only to realise they've given what's precious to the pigs...They end up bruised and broken and my heart breaks because all they wanted was to connect on a deep level. That's why we need Jesus because all of us are spiritually wired for connection on a deep level, that yearning to trust completely is a need only God can meet. God's love letters to us...the Psalms 42 v 7 tell us deep calls to deep... Princess, real intimacy can't be rushed, it's a risky business. Real intimacy takes time because trust takes time. For your heart's sake recognise who you are allowing into your inner world and only reveal your precious layers one at a time over a period of time.

You are precious... so treat yourself with the value of your worth, princess, and build friendships over time and with great care.

Take 5: think of 5 people who have helped you see your preciousness and worth and pray God would encourage them in whatever they are doing right now.

Proverbs 31 v 10 "*She is more precious than rubies, who can compare to her?*"

[1]Proverbs 4 v 23
[2]Mathew 7 v 6

Drop 41 ~ Judgment

There is nothing that will blind you more than the pride of your own opinion. In Matthew 7 v1-5, Jesus explains how the sin of a judgmental attitude can blind your eyes. It is so easy to look at someone and make a snap judgment on how things appear, we've all done it. Did you know that this is a sin with serious consequences? When we judge someone we are saying that we know better than the Lord God Almighty. Think about that for a mo… a human person knowing more than He who sees ALL things, knows ALL things and is in ALL situations at any given time…Mmm… Judging another is pure foolishness because we can never have the perfect perspective of God.

No human being can see into another person's heart, this is a simple fact. We can interpret a person's heart from the behaviour which flows out from it and measuring the talk with walk; but we never really know what's on the inside. Beloved, we can become blind to our own glaring imperfections because our minds are so taken up with finding fault in another brother or sister. Do you know how this grieves the Father? Only God can see why any particular person feels, thinks and acts as they do. Only He has journeyed their life with them and walked in their shoes. Only He knows the reasons for the glaring inconstancy of human nature. So we should let Him do the judging!

Another aspect of judging is that it places you on the side of sin which of course places your focus from a position of darkness. When we make snap judgments we stop thinking in a God perspective. When we judge another person we take our eyes off the big picture and get distracted by often insignificant details. In the journey that is this life we've got mountains to climb and valleys to negotiate; we need all the vision we can get. By taking time to talk things through with God we can express our frustrations without sinning. By talking with Him we can get encouragement and a new vision for a person, place or thing!

Take a few moments - when did you last judge? Don't beat yourself up about it, we've all done it and probably will in the future but… Before you go through any more of this day ask God to forgive you and the Holy Spirit to put an alarm bell in your head for next time you wander down a judgmental path.

Isaiah 33 v 22 *"For the Lord is our Judge and He alone is our lawgiver."*

Drop 42 ~ Eyes to see

Read about Elisha (2 Kings 6 v 15-17). Allow me to give you a bit of background to this story, it's really cool! Elisha is God's prophet at a time when the Moabite and the Aramean armies are at war with Israel. There's a famine and drought and it's all a bit of a hairy time. However, many, many times Elisha demonstrates his utter faith in God and many miraculous things happen. Elisha helps the Israelite King in his military manoeuvres and spiritual walk and because of this Israel is greatly helped.

Can you imagine what it would be like to wake up and find yourself surrounded by a bloodthirsty mob? I don't think I could have been as self assured as Elisha. However he had built up such a relationship of trust and faith in God that he is unfazed. WAOW! He's like 'chill, it's totally cool, God will sort this out, I'm His child and He's my God and my eyes are open!'

Elisha was so in tune with the Spirit of God that he saw with his spiritual eyes rather than his natural; because of this he was able to see beyond the obvious. He prayed the spiritual blindness of his servant would be removed so he could see from the perspective of Heaven. The very thing that scared his servant he took hold of in prayer and used as their weapon of escape. Princess what scares you? What holds you in its grip? Did you know you can take that fear and use it to good effect in prayer to take captive that which seeks to overwhelm you? What are the areas in you world today where you feel there's no way out? Think about that because if you're going to overcome something you need to look that sucker in the eye. Yep it might be a big problem, a huge one, but you are the child of an even bigger, even greater God.

Open your eyes, girlfriend, you are a force to be reckoned with just like Elisha. Pray for God to be creative in you, to show you areas of blindness in your own faith. Develop a relationship of trust and power in Christ then look around you and laugh… there are many more with you than those threatening to harm you. Have eyes to see babe, it's not how it appears…

Go and lick all of Psalm 121; it's so cool…it's like a big ice cream on a hot day!

Psalm 91 v 9 *"If you make the Most High your dwelling - the Lord, who is our refuge- then no harm will befall you, no disaster will come near your tent for He will command His angels concerning you to guard you in all your way's they will lift you up so that you do not strike your foot against a rock."*

Drop 43 ~ Stepping stone moments

We're not meant to stay standing on a stepping stone, did you know that? It's a place of transitional time limited waiting. It's the place you use for a moment to get you to the solid ground. Sometimes in life, we find ourselves on a stepping stone and it can feel very precarious, particularly if it's covered in moss! Sometimes life feels very wobbly and we might even wonder if we're going to make it to that nice dry bank on the other side. When you're in that place usually there's fast water, isn't there, swirling and bubbling around your very inappropriate footwear. (How many times have you wished you'd worn your humble practical wellies rather than flip flops, eh?)

There may be times when you may feel like you've taken a side step in life rather than the progress you so desperately wanted; and there are times when you can find yourself being somewhere you'd never have chosen: you know… those times when you set out on a course of action feeling certain it was the right thing, only to wobble in the flow and question if you ever 'heard' from God at all!

Do you know what I think, I think *how* we see these temporary places of stone really matters. You can see it as provision for the next step to something more certain. You can praise God he didn't ask you to make that huge jump from one side to the other in one go? OR you can look at your feet and give in to despair; I know I've done all of the above!

The point I suppose I'm trying to make is that times of uncertainty will happen; we will feel vulnerable and precarious as we find our path through life. But we have a God who has planned each of our steps.[1] He who is faithful no matter how we see things and has given us countless promises of our security in Him.[2]

If you're feeling like you've side stepped rather than moved forward or you're in a wobbly place, I really want to encourage you to try and see things from another perspective. Try this for size… just imagine that when you look back over your life all the side steps, all the back and forward steps intertwine. Slow… slow… quick… quick… slow. Now picture you're fox-trotting through life with the King of Kings and actually dancing not wobbling in the arms of your beloved... Mmmm… how good does that feel?

Psalm 40 v 1-3 *"I waited patiently for the Lord; He turned to me and heard my cry; He lifted me out of the slimy pit, out of the mud and the mire. He set my feet upon a rock and gave me a firm place to stand. He put a new song in my mouth, a hymn of praise to our God, many will see and fear and put their trust in the Lord.*"

Go and encourage your soul with Psalm 27, bless you Hunny bun!

[1]Psalm 37 v 23-24
[2]John 10 v 28

Drop 44 ~ Raw material

You have everything you need to do what you gotta do in your life time, only it may not always feel or seem like it. God has put something unique into you that only you can do and His promise to you is that He will equip those He calls... and honey if you're breathing, you're called! I have been reading the story of when Jesus fed the five thousand recently. It challenged me in that there were a few basic things He required to carry out this task.

a) Prayer... in that He gave thanks as He honoured His Father, knowing that everything comes from Him. In doing this he gives God the Father 1st place in his life. God calls us to do the same. We must lay aside everything and put God first. If we want to see the miraculous provision of God today we need to pray. If Jesus lived it so must we.

b) Raw material... in that He required something from those he was serving. It wasn't a lot, just a couple of fish and some bread. You may not feel like you have very much to offer God in terms of who you are or what you have; all He requires is our wee bit....of raw material! The amazing thing is that no matter how low, inadequate or weak we feel God our Father has made up the deficit. All He asks is that we do our bit obediently. Are you feeling inadequate, like your raw material isn't enough? If you are, know that He will equip you for whatever He asks of you.

c) Compassion.... his heart was moved with compassion for these people. We need to seek God's heart on issues in our lives. We need a heart just like Jesus. In our multi media world our hearts can so easily become desensitised to God's heart and become hardened to the anguished cries from the throne room of Heaven. I'm ashamed to say I often watch the news and read the paper and am untouched by the pain of others. There are some horrendous events unfolding in this world as I write and you read this book. I have to remind myself these are real lives, real folks like you and me suffering awful atrocities. How can our response be to put the kettle on rather than fall on our knees... Ouch!

Gosh there's so much I don't know about theology and all the God stuff, but I do know this - prayer works. If Jesus modelled so much of it we need to follow His lead... I'm convicted as I write this because I genuinely do care about people, they matter to me. I really do hurt for people who are in pain and it matters...so I'm challenged because I can get so wrapped up in my own world I neglect to pray as I should. Girls, let's use the raw material God has placed within each one of us and ask

Him to reveal His heart to us that we may align our hearts with His. Now I'm gonna make a list, a time and pray…!

Can you take some time to pray or offer some raw materials like finance or skill to God this week?

2 Chronicles 7 v 14 & 15 *"If my people who are called by name will humble themselves and pray and seek my face and turn form their wicked ways, then I will hear from heaven and will forgive their sin and heal their land. Now my eyes will be open and my ears attentive to the prayers offered in this place…"*

Drop 45 ~ Who loves ya, baby?

When I was a little girl there used to be a programme called Kojak on TV. The strap line of the main character was "Who loves ya baby?" I never understood it at the time to be honest... Anyway, I was thinking about this for some reason when it struck me how we can be defined by our other half. (I was single for a long time so all you princesses who don't want or haven't yet met your knight bear with me, there is a point.) My Husband, my Parents and kids love me; I might even have a few friends who'd admit to loving me too. But the defining love of my life is my Jesus… my saviour - come on sing it with me… Nah only joking!!! *Darleen if this ever gets published and you read this... you rock and I love that song really!* You see, my reality is that Jesus really is the love of my life!

Are you satisfied to be loved on a human level only? If you are, you are missing the whole point of your 'Christianity'. Jesus wants to be the first in your heart. He longs to show you the intimacy of true love, perfect love in Him. He's a jealous lover who is so totally passionate about you, he will give you the very best of his love. If you allow his gentle yet life changing love into your heart you will see that there is simply no comparison to what any man can give you. Jesus is in this relationship for the long haul not just a fling. As someone once said he wants a bride not a girlfriend!

Anyway Babe, I wonder who you think loves you today. The Bible says the Lord has set His affection on you. The Lord has loved you with an everlasting love, keeping His covenant of love to a thousand generations to those who love Him and keep His commands.[1] You are no accident, the fact that you are completely and wholly loved by God is a purposed and deliberate thing. He has chosen you, yes you, to set his affections upon. Wow!! If you've come to that point where you realise you're not perfect, yep… like the rest of us, a sinner and really want to enter deep into relationship with God then be blessed, girlfriend! You are indeed a new person in Christ. Not only that but you have joy and security because you know whose you are!

If you let him, He will show you unconditional and humble love like you've never known. Jesus said in John 3 v 29 "*The bride belongs to the bridegroom. The friend who attends the bridegroom waits and listens for him, and is full of joy when he hears the bridegroom's voice. That joy is mine and it is now complete.*" When you say yes to Jesus' love over any other you simply make his joy complete! In the light of this love what is your response going to be? Why not dive into this ocean of abundant love, yes it will have its costs, like making time to get to be intimate through prayer and listening; but the price *you* pay will seem like nothing compared to what you get back.

Psalm 42 v 7 Paraphrased… "*Deep love calls me into its depths I yearn to find its perfect love as I dive into the flow… into the exhilarating roar of your waterfalls. I am abandoned to wave after wave of love sweeping over me afresh.*"

[1]Psalm 103 v 17

Drop 46 ~ Agonising over past events

Ever been at an event only to come home and mull over the conversations you've had with people? Then that mulling turns to analysing and the analysing turns to worry... You think about how you were perceived and whether or not you caused offence... You wonder if the fact that someone narked you showed? Oh dear, oh dear... You know I think we've all done that at times, haven't we? We've all hit the re-run button of the recording in our head and poured over past events particularly where it matters how we were perceived!

One of the most painful things to experience is the pain of misunderstanding. You know, when you're genuine and you know the intentions of your heart are pure and kind only for them to be perceived in another way. God sees the intentions of your heart; He understands your every motive, pure and not so pure...but you know I believe God is more concerned with how we look on the inside than the out. If you've been misunderstood and know that pain, take it to Him. He always understands and will always work in the situation if you can have the character to invite Him to work on your behalf. (Be warned, butting out requires a lot of character and patience!) Trust in the knowledge that when life is over He's the only one you have to impress.

If you're finding that you have a re-run player in your head, there is a STOP button which only you can press. Choose to talk to you best friend (Jesus) and trust that you are secure in Him. He thinks you're fabulous, not just ok! Sadly, too many of us allow past events to shape our futures. Sister of mine in Christ, FIGHT for this to not be the case in your life! Battles are lost and won in the arena of the mind. Choose every day to exercise the discipline of control over the negativity and rubbish that floats so easily into the mind. God has promised you that you are a new creation in Him.[1] You are wholly loved and valued by Him.[2] Start speaking a new language, confidently positive in your amazing God. This is the day that He has made for you. So don't be satisfied and distracted. Don't focus on the yesterdays. Girlfriend, God is big enough to cover you where there have been misunderstood. Know this day, you're designed for success and that means walking face forward not backward.

Don't do re-runs, what's happened has happened; live for today in the knowledge it's a brand new day and you're God's girl!

Psalm 123 v 1 *"I lift up my eyes to you, to you whose throne is in heaven."*

[1]2 Cor 5 v 17
[2]Song of Songs 2 v 4

Drop 47 ~ <u>There's a time to say no</u>

Do you have days where you feel like you get out of bed and wade through treacle just to get to the kitchen and even then the effort of making a cuppa seems more than you can do? Girlfriends, if you feel like this know that you're not meant to unless there's a reason like illness… We are not meant to just make it through but sadly many of us are so overloaded we're drowning. Well babe here's a life-line…learn to say no! The lovely thing about Christians is that we genuinely love others and want to help, but if we're so overstretched that there's no life in our life then this is wrong.

Life is a juggling act and it's good to be stretched but it's important to be led by God in that process rather than driven by ideas. A good idea needs to be a God idea! God requires hard work from us and it's brill because when we're being led by Him there's a kind of satisfaction and life in His work.[1] When we try and do what seems best to us we become exhausted and disillusioned.

Because in our Western culture we try and cram so much into our world, our dreams can be drowned out in the din of business and joy robbed from what should be a pleasure. Sometimes expectations can pressure us but if they are not from God, they are ropes with which we tie ourselves in knots! We need to allow God to prioritise our lives and order our steps. It's amazing what will seem less/more important as we involve the Lord. Anyway girlfriend the point is you have the right to say, "Sorry I can't, I'm busy…" If you're too busy to enjoy the journey, maybe you need to look at what you've chosen to cram into your world.

We often derive our value from what we do for Christ rather than who we are in Christ! It's the classic Mary and Martha struggle.[1] But, you know what, if we are to be firstly God pleasers, we need to learn to sometimes say no. Because you're a lovely person and I believe you are, it's easy to get caught up serving people rather than God. Serving people is a worthy and noble task and we must have a servant's heart if we are going to be useful to God's kingdom. We need to make our time with God top priority in our day; it should come before any acts of service. Whatever we do will only be useful if it's born out of deep intimacy with the only one who is able to give it power and purpose.

Princess, when was the last time you made - *and yes you have to make it* - time for yourself to sit and be still? When was the last time you rested in God and allowed Him to set the agenda for your day? Take a half an hour to be still before the one who loves you most. Unplug the phone, get rid of distractions and listen…We're not too good at this, but try anyway… light a candle, hide the clock if you have to, but close your eyes and listen, for God has something important to say to you about your future. Hunny bun, your dreams are relevant, useful to the kingdom of God; can I beg you today to audit your world. Are there things you need to say no to for a season?

Just stop for a moment take a big breath in fill your lungs full and listen to the air. Now put your feet up on a coffee table or small child, put down the book, take 5 and…breathe…

[1]Matthew 11 v 28-30

Drop 48 ~ And a time to say, Yeah baby!

God has a specific task on this earth, at this time in history that only you can accomplish. I can't do it because I'm not you and you can't do what God needs me to do because... you're not me! Sometimes we wait for 'a word' or a feeling before we act upon the dreams of our heart. Only you can live your dreams babe! In psychology there's a paradigm called bystander apathy; simply put it's where people see action needs to be taken but they stand around passively inactive because they think someone else will do it. Sadly the church is full of bystanders and apathetic ones at that. Some of this is down to lack of vision or release by leadership but much of it is down to simple laziness on our part! In our comfortable Western culture we've just gotten too, well, comfortable. It's too easy to sleepwalk into church on a Sunday, back into 'life' on Monday.

I believe there's a groaning, birthing of new men and women who are crying out to be released to kick ass on earth. There's a rumbling in our not so distant future where the men and women of God are going to have to waken up from slumber. I believe the times of cosy Christianity are drawing to a close and we're going to have to increasingly take a stand for justice and truth based on the Bible. Yes there are times to take stock and evaluate your motives, and auditing our spiritual world should be a lifestyle we develop, but… when that's done we need to get on with the job at hand.

You may think you've no special purpose but if you have breath in your body God needs you to be YOU in all the fullness of who you are. If you're a lollypop lady do it for Christ; pray for each person you walk across the road, smile at them, jump in the puddles and love what you do. If you're a mum gossip the gospel at the school gate, be interested in the needs of others and reach out in love. If you're a leader, lead with the diligence, humility, holiness and courage of Christ. Get real…and model real gutsy, vulnerable Jesus loving Christianity like you mean it.

Girlfriend, no one else can do what you can do. So just say YES to God…You have been fitted and shaped by the creator himself…you are amazing. He has equipped you for what He has called you do.[1]

John 15 v 16 *"You did not choose me but I chose you and appointed you to go and bear fruit – fruit that will last...."*

Just say Yeah Baby Yeah… Now go look up!

[1]Hebrews 13 v20-21

Drop 49 ~ Don't sell yourself short

In our culture it's not the done thing to admit to being good at anything. How often have you heard someone say "Gosh it was nothing"? There's a kinda false humility here that implies a lack of value to what we do. Girlfriend this is wrong! God wants us to walk in humility, it's vitally important if are going to learn from him but He also wants us to walk in truth. When you've worked your butt off and accomplished something it's ok to feel a sense of achievement in a job well done. You can enjoy knowing God's satisfaction in seeing you accomplish goals, knowing the glory goes to Him.

The Bible says whatever you do, do it to the glory of God.[1] At times it's tempting to undervalue what we do in our day to day life. I truly believe that when we are living for God all we do matters to Him. So often He has shown me something totally profound while I'm cleaning the bath or cutting the grass. So don't allow the ordinariness of life rob you of your extraordinariness in Christ. You see, babe, when you are in partnership with the Holy Spirit, He can help you to accomplish things beyond your wildest dreams. He can be your encouragement when you've messed up, your strength when you're weary and your hope in the midst of discouragement.

Another wonderful aspect of God's design for our journey is that we partner with others as we walk. This is such a pain at times and yet such a real privilege. There's a scene at the end of 'Lord of the Rings' where Frodo and his companions have been through their worst nightmare and have come through against all odds. They're in the pub and no words are spoken between them but their faces say it all. They didn't ask for the path their lives took, but they embraced it, learning character and wisdom along the way. They know their achievement, they know what's happened and all they've accomplished and they are satisfied.

Don't sell yourself short, princess, because one day we will sit around another table, we will look around at the faces of our comrades, we will know the deep satisfaction of a job well done, despite the odds and we will hear the Master's voice say, "Well done good and faithful servant." [2]

Ephesians 2 v 10 "For we are God's workmanship, created in Christ Jesus to do good works, which God prepared in advance for us to do."

[1] 1 Cor 10 v 31
[2] Matthew 25 v 21

Drop 50 ~ Word up!

Have you ever said something only to do a re-take in your mind and think did I just say that? The Bible has a lot to say about how we use words… get this lot from proverbs… *12 v 25 "An anxious heart weighs a man down, but a kind word builds him up"; 13 v 2 "From the fruit of his lips a man enjoys good things…" & V 3 "He who guards his lips guards his life…"; 15 v 4 "The tongue that brings healing is a tree of life, but a hurtful tongue crushes the spirit."*

Princess what comes out of our mouths matters to God. It tells us in James 3 that the tongue simply sets the course for our journey in this life. Do you want your life to be full of goodness or sour grapes? We need to not only live lives worthy of Christ but use mouths worthy of Christ. I try very hard to watch what slips out of my mouth because it really does betray what's really going on inside the soul. That's what's really important here, because if my talk has an effect on my walk I need it to be a positive life giving force. Sadly there are many times when I know my talk has not brought forth life.

Do you know that when we use words to negative effect that we grieve the Holy Spirit? Gosh I'm so convicted as I write this…You see in the privacy of my own home I do grumble my frustrations out. Perhaps you too have had times when you have had a good old grumble about your leadership or your children…? Girls *(and I'm preaching to myself 1st)* grumbling is simply veiled pride. It's a lack of appreciation for the provision of God. You may be very justified in your frustrations but God needs us to get in line with His way of doing things. He tells us "do not grumble against each other".[1]

The problem with words are, once they've been spoken we can't undo them… They're out there for all to see. So let's try very hard to watch what slips out of our mouths because it really determines the direction we'll go in. Be encouraged, if we can cultivate a beautiful mouth perhaps with the Holy Spirit's help we can cultivate a beautiful soul!

Ephesians 4 v 29 *"Do not let unwholesome talk come out of your mouths, but only what is helpful for building others up according to their needs, that it may benefit those who listen."*

Go read James 3 v 1-12…

[1]James 5 v 9

Drop 51 ~ Would ya risk it?

I'm pants at taking risks. By nature I'm quite a timid person and while there's a part of me that can do up front stuff there's a bigger part of me that cringes when I have to talk on a one to one. I worry that the conversation will dry up, or that I'll come across as weird or needy. The vulnerabilities of my character get particularly bad at that time of the month! Can I hear an Amen?

However if we are going to achieve our potential in life honey bun, ***we've got to ruthlessly fight the nagging self doubt in our mind if we're going to live in the freedom of Christ***. Read that again. In the moments of *yuckness* when we feel at our most pathetic, it's in those moments wars are won and lost from the inside out. Clawing over the barriers of our soul is liberating... but gosh getting over can be so very hard. Sweetheart it's not easy to reach out and comfort another when you're hurting yourself. It takes great courage to risk humility when already feeling humiliated. It takes great love to risk rejection, again. It takes great sacrifice to achieve when all the odds are stacked against you.

I started today's bit by saying I'm not into risks but I'm praying for the sake of my spiritual footprint upon this earth that God helps me in this area. I pray that the Holy Spirit will strengthen me to love with such a passion that I'll risk everything. I am convinced the reward is worth the risk, it's just really tough trying to get over the obstacles in my character to get there; but I am determined to.

If you look back in history you'll see that those who achieved amazing feats didn't think they were very amazing at the time. Go 'google' Hudson Taylor, Elizabeth Fry, George Muller, Rosa Parks or Mother Teresa to be inspired by their accomplishments. They were vulnerable people who had all the same doubts and worries we do but they ruthlessly pressed on. They clawed through and had victory from the inside out!

If the thought of risky living ruffles your feathers, pray about it; God needs you in this game and time is short. He is cool about your fears and will help you through them. He is always faithful and will never ask you to do anything He hasn't prepared in advance for you. Go on risk it… You can do all things because the Holy Spirit, the power of God Himself, lives within you!

"Know that great love and great achievements involve great risk." Anon

1 Thessalonians 3 v 13 "*May He strengthen your hearts so that you will be blameless and holy in the presence of our God the Father when our Lord Jesus comes with all His holy ones.*"

Drop 52 ~ The reality gap

Oh gosh… God has placed this day's theme so strongly on my heart that I can feel the depth of hurt you feel towards God in this area. Mmmm… I take this very seriously because I truly know you are so precious...

We are all people of dreams which is a wonderful thing, I believe it demonstrates the creative force of the human spirit. Your dreams may not be huge and exciting or perhaps they are; but whatever they are, they are yours and that makes them valuable! Somehow we have to live out these dreams in the reality of a fallen and corrupted world: a world of logic and order in some instances but confused and irrational in others.

I met a lady once who after much prayer, sold her home and bought a Christian bookshop. She dreamed that it would impact the lives of people in that town. She sourced local churches and was assured of their support, it all looked rosy. But after five years of struggling it went into receivership and she financially lost everything. My heart broke for her as she told me of her disappointment in the Lord for allowing it to happen. The despair she felt tipped her into disillusionment in her relationship with Christ.

Have you ever felt like that? Like you've given up everything and God's let you down? If you have you've hit one of the most pivotal moments in your journey with God. The reality Gap, Jesus hit it on the cross when he cried out "My God, my God why have you forsaken me"? Babe, when the reality of awfulness hits the passion of your dream head-on it hurts like hell.

Oh princess, I hope you believe I'm not trotting out trite words as I write this. I have known this pain of utter disappointment in my own life and there are no words when you're right in the gap. It's when you're in the gap you have to make a choice. You choose to continue to trust in God in spite of the pain. When you're in the gap, the dross of self inspired love gets burned away and something like pure gold is left behind. It's in the gap battles are lost and won…

Know this, you do not enter the gap alone, when you've poured yourself out for a cause like a drink offering and it seems all your efforts are wasted, Jesus knows.[1] When your dreams or expectations are crushed by the reality of circumstance, Jesus knows. Sweetheart, he more than knows, he cares; he cares deeply with the same passionate love that drinks bitter disappointment when one of his children walks away.

So how do you survive the Reality Gap? I've found if you're going to get better and not bitter, it's vital to speak to your spirit. It's vital to remind your heart that God is love; He loves you despite how it may seem. God will work the situation to glory if you surrender to His will, hard as it is. If there was another way He'd do it like a shot. (Don't you think He'd have whipped His own Son off the cross if there was another way?) I really believe He allows not one of His children to endure pain lightly. He loves us too much.

He loves with such a passion that he gave His all for you. As a father, to watch your child tortured must be harder than going through it yourself, but He did that and some. He catches each one of your precious tears in a bottle and holds them so close in His heart. Child, He feels your pain as you cry out in anger and frustration. His shoulders are big enough to take the battering of our human perspective as He waits to reveal the why in the fullness of time.[2] This is real love.

I know when I've come through the reality gap and have seen the greater picture, God was right in the gap with me, helping me to grow up. I sure do have some whopper scars but they are marks of encouragement to others because I made it through the gap. It was messy and often my attitude was totally sinful, but I made it all the same and so can you! If you've been in the gap you need to recognise your wounding and give yourself time to heal. Read the Bible, look up the scriptures below and remind yourself of God's love. Go and get someone to pray with you, it'll probably take more than once! Know you're growing and you can more than overcome the gap, you can one day dance on it.

It's worth noting here, that often *we* are the ones who define or choose our expectations. When we try and say how God should behave or act in a situation, what we're really saying is not thy will be done but, *my* will be done.... Ouch! As Christians our goal is to love like Christ.[3] The love that says even though I find it hard to see how anything good can ever come out of this situation, I have set my course and I'm not letting go. I choose to love even though there's nothing in it for me. I think this love, this unspeakably noble love, is why Jesus looked on the world and just couldn't walk away and leave us in our own mess. He saw the stark reality of our hopelessness in a world of sin. Babe can I encourage you if you're in the gap, don't bail, hang on in there. You will make it through...

Bless you, you've done so well, the outworking of your dreams lies with the dream caster and He loves you. His way of accomplishing the dream may be very different to ours. Someone once said Christianity is very simple. It's God will, God's way, for God's glory...

"Thy will be done as it is in Heaven."[4]

[1]Phil 2 v 17 [2]Eccl 8 v 6 [3]John 15 v 9-14 [4]Matthew 6 v 9-15

Words of hope for crushed expectations...

Isaiah 50 v 7 *"Because the Sovereign Lord helps me, I will not be disgraced. Therefore I have set my face like flint and I know I will not be put to shame."*

Psalm 40 v 1-3 *"I waited patiently for the Lord; He turned to me and heard my cry. He lifted me out of the slimy pit, out of the mud and mire; and set my feet on a rock and gave me a firm place to stand. He put a new song in my mouth, a hymn of praise to our God. Many will see and fear and put their trust in the Lord."*

Psalm 118 v 5 *"In my anguish I cried out to the Lord, and He answered me, by setting me free."*

Drop 53 ~ Pondering

In the first chapter of Luke's gospel it tells us about the events surrounding Mary the mother of Jesus. Although very young she was thrust into centre stage and lots of life-changing events unfolded very fast, perhaps too fast… She had a lot of adjustments to make in her world as her role and identity changed.

I don't know about you but if too many things change at once in my world I tend to feel overwhelmed. I was thinking about my response and Mary's response. Like Mary, I had my first child when I was quite young. Like Mary, having a baby at that time was a surprise and lots of things started to rapidly change in my world over which I had no control. Ever felt like things are changing too fast and there's no way you can slow 'em down? My response to becoming pregnant was guilt and fear and many tears as I faced many future uncertainties as a lone parent.

Mary in contrast was so deeply rooted in relationship with God that she pondered. She just sat down in a quite place and pondered. Wow…what a woman! I would define this type of pondering as 'a peaceful place in the mind into which your circumstance is enveloped in the certainty of a loving God'. It's only when we step out of chaos and into the arms of God that we can get the ability to ponder. And I'll tell ya something else girlfriend, it takes maturity to recognise when you need to go and get with God for a ponderin'!!

When we ponder we afford God the opportunity of breathing His creative life into our person. It's in the ponderin' that we hear Him whisper words of hope, direction and perspective. Do you need to make time today to consider your world, the people who've influenced you, the circumstances which have shaped you? Then ask God to help ponder these things in Him. He has life inspiring encouragement and purpose to reveal to you in your place of pondering.

Could your world do with a bit of ponderin' today?

Psalm 111 v 2 *"Great are the works of the Lord; they are pondered by all who delight in them."*

Drop 54 ~ Jargon

So often we 'talk the talk' don't we? We use words like 'love', 'freedom', 'grace', 'peace' ... or we use clichés like 'a servant's heart' or 'my sister in Christ'. Like anything else in life these words roll off the tongue depending on the company we're in... like spiritual jargon...

(Oxford dictionary) Jargon......

"Words or expressions developed for use within a particular group or profession; sounding ugly and unintelligible to the outsider." OUCH!! I want my words to be beautiful, life bringing, not ugly and unintelligible... and I certainly don't want to shut people out. Girlfriend, I think we need to be very careful to model how we talk Gods talk don't you?

Here's what the Bible says about God's word: Genesis 1...God spoke and creation was born; 2 Samuel 22 v 31 ... the words of the Lord are flawless; Psalm 119 v 105 ... God's word is a lamp to our feet... They bring life and fruitfulness; Isaiah 40 v 8... the word of our God stands forever. God's words bring life; Luke 6 v 45 Message Bible "It's who you are, not what you say, that counts. Your true being brims over into true words and deeds."

Ask yourself do my words bring life; are they beautiful, creative, and simple? We sooo... need to be honest and humble, to speak from our heart and not in clichés. If you're a Christian and find yourself jargoning, go and suck a lemon till the operant conditioning works! If we're doing this thing right anyone should be able to understand us, but more than that people should know who are by the way we live. There's no point shabba-dabba-do-ing in church on a Sunday if you act like a stuck up cow the rest of the week. Someone once said if you take care of the walk, the talk will take care of itself.

In my enthusiasm as a young Christian I'm sure I was unbearable in this area *(perhaps I still am but people are too gracious to tell me!)*. I was so desperate to prove God was at work in me, that I spoke in lingo; now when I think about it I totally cringe!! Babe, you keep being you because the truth is, jargon is for posers and God needs real people. How you live will say it for you and who you are is good enough. Don't be intimidated or too impressed by others into being anything other than real. We're called to walk in truth and when we do we allow space for others to walk in truth too. The only person we ever have to impress is God and He's already nuts about you!

Pray – ask the Holy Spirit to put a flashing light bulb in your head and make it go off when you step out of truth and into jargon!

1 Corinthians 2 v 13 *"This is what we speak, not in words taught to us by humans, but words taught by the Holy Spirit, expressing spiritual truths in spiritual words."*

Drop 55 ~ The ultimate power walkers

In the book of Joshua in the Bible Ch 5 v 13 – 6 v 20 (*go and read it, it's a totally cool story*) the Israelites without realising it were psyching out the city of Jericho. They had no tactics other than obedience to God and couldn't have known the terrifying effect their marching was having on the people inside. As far as they were concerned they could have simply been making themselves look stupid.

They might have wondered if their leader Joshua was off his trolley or if they were all on a secret fitness plan from eating too much manna and needing to shed a few pounds. Imagine walking around the walls of the city or area you live in. I'm sure in Joshua's time it would easily have been a good five or six miles. Imagine having to get up, do your chores, sort out the evening meal, then pack up and go for the day's hike. I reckon you'd be pretty cheesed off, not to mention knackered. The Israelite people had to do this again and again and again…for 6 days. AND just when they thought the job was done they had to do it all over again like a final great push… … and walk around another 7 times. Phew…!

I want to draw out a couple of points for us to ponder on…
When we walk in obedience to God and our leadership we may look stupid. I'm smiling as I write this, hasn't God got the best sense of humour? Not only does obedience keep us walking in humility it allows Gods word "He chooses the foolish things of this earth to confound the wise"[1] to take form and life. If I'm honest I hope it gives God a laugh at times too, He carries so much of our junk He's entitled to a laugh at our expense!

Anyway chick, to get back to the point… **We may not look as stupid as we think we do.** You see walking in obedience affords us protection and blessing. In fact when we're walking in obedience we psyche out the powers of hell. They are caught because time is coming to an end and their destruction is imminent. Ultimately when God's plans are revealed, obedience will show great faith and a maturity in relationship with God.

When we do it God's way mighty things are accomplished through very ordinary methods. Walking is a pretty ordinary thing isn't it? In Exodus the people had to walk and walk hard, it was no picnic. They had to focus and get on with the job albeit a simple one, praise and walk, then praise and walk some more… Be encouraged when we persevere in the ordinariness of life walking in submission and obedience we will accomplish great things!

I believe just like the Israelites we often have no idea of what God is up to as we walk through life until He's been and done it! So despise not the little things, the seemingly ordinary things because when we walk, praise then walk some more we are the ultimate power walkers!

"We need to sacrifice ourselves in the natural, so that the supernatural can become natural in us." (Oswald Chambers)

Jeremiah 6 v16 *"Stand at the cross roads and look for the ancient paths…ask where is the good way and walk in it."*

[1]Cor 1 v 27

Drop 56 ~ Danger - unauthorised zone!

My mind is like one of those wee fireflies Walt Disney had in his films. It flits from one thought to another and is kinda all over the place. Are you similar? Women tend to think in a more spaghetti type way with flowing tangents of thought all over the place, it's one of the aspects of our wonderfulness! I've found myself thinking of a happy thing only to go off on a tangent and cry because I remember something especially poignant. Perhaps when I finish writing this I'll have time to go and get some professional help. I was at a spaghetti junction in my mind the other day and found myself entering an amber zone. I had started to think about someone who had wronged me and started to judge them and resent them in my heart, which lead me wondering down a bad path…ouch!

Sweet cheeks, there's another more dangerous side to mind hopping, however, that I want to focus on and I'm speaking to myself as I write this. I've found there are danger Zones in the mind we can stray into... Zones which take us from a green to amber to red alert level in the spirit and they're not a coincidence. Here's an example; your husband has been grumpy and had particularly bad breath for the last few weeks. You sit down to ponder, pray whatever and you find yourself thinking how non-smelly and nice the new praise and worship leader is…DANGER! Want another? There are loads… You are waiting in a queue at the cinema and you see a colleague's 16 year old daughter heavily pregnant, do you jump to self satisfaction or judgementalism, even gossip…? Do you see where I'm going with this?

The Bible tells us to take captive every thought[1] and filter and proactively choose what we focus on. This then will shape your soul.[2] It's vital if we're not going to land ourselves in the middle of a destructive red zone that we recognise the alert of our own conscience. We have the power to take captive every thought and resist the devil but… there is a precondition for our ability to do this. We are required to submit to God, to surrender and humble ourselves before Him so that we can have His power. So, taking control over what's bouncing around in our heads takes us to be walking out life submitted and humble.

A long time ago I prayed the Holy Spirit would put a big alarm in my head which could go off when I enter a danger Zone. The wonder of it is He did and I praise God for it. You see I'm a bit of a putz; at times I don't see the problem till I'm fighting the fire. The truth is we all get through life in spite of our own ability to wander near or off the edge of the cliff. Why not ask the Holy Spirit to give you your own virus scanning system in the computer of your mind, then your spaghetti type wanderings will have built in protection!

Psalm 19 v 12-14 *"Who can discern their errors? Forgive my hidden faults. Keep your servant from wilful sins; may they not rule over me. Then I will be blameless, innocent of great transgressions. May the words of my mouth and the meditations of my heart be pleasing in your sight, O Lord my Rock and my Redeemer."*

[1]2 Cor 10 v 5 [2]Phil 4 v 8

Drop 57 ~ Leading

When I was preparing this I had the picture of an arrow, and it struck me that the point that takes the maximum impact is the head. In our churches it is those in leadership who are at the cutting edge point of the arrow. They are the ones who break the ground so to speak and if you've ever led anything you'll know what I mean. Being the person at the point of impact is often a very painful and lonely place to be. (Not a lot of surface area on an arrow point.)

In our nation, in our churches we have become cynical and mistrusting of those in leadership. It's true many of those called to positions of responsibility have let us down badly and tried to use the devil's tools to build the Kingdom. However there are many more doing a fabulous job and getting tarred with the same brush. This strikes me not so much as unfair, but ungodly. If God holds leaders in high esteem so should we. We should make their job as easy as we can by not criticising and judging them with our demi-god standards. They are human too! And the same standard you judge by will be the measure God uses against you, so beware.

God either is in control of the world or He isn't, if you believe God is sovereign despite how life looks then He knows what He's doing. There may be awful governments in power, there may be even worse church leaders but by behaving in a righteous way under their leadership brings glory to God.[1] I have tested this principle and know it to be true.

I hope you get my heart on this because we must take a stand against injustice, but *how* we take that stand will bring either victory or defeat in a kingdom sense. David's story is a wonderful example of someone who respected God's choice of authority in King Saul (see Sam. 20). He modelled the way of victory despite such unjust behaviour from his leader Saul. In spite of great provocation he refused to speak or act in an ungodly way about Saul. Very few leaders in this nation will try to throw a spear at your head and for every awful one I'm sure there are many more genuinely lovely people who are doing *their utmost for His highest*, to coin a phrase. We owe it to our leaders to pray for them and ensure that they have the time they need with God. We do them a service to release them to this and they do us a service to take it.

Who has God placed in leadership over you? Enquire after them and commit yourself to blessing them abundantly and cover them continually in prayer…

Hebrews 13 v 17 "*Obey your leaders and submit to their authority. They keep watch over you as men who must give an account. Obey them so that their work will be a joy, not a burden, for that would be of no advantage to you.*"

Drop 58 ~ The protection of fear

Fear of the Lord inspires obedience - Deut 5 v 29 *"Oh that their hearts would be inclined to fear me and keep all my commands, so that it might go well with their children for ever."* God's longing is to bless us and keep us safe, but He also knows His power enough to know we should fear it.

The fear of God is the beginning of wisdom.[1] Why is that…? Why is fear the prerequisite to wisdom? I think it's because it keeps our perspective in the truth of who God really is. He is a God of justice who fights ferociously for those He loves. He is a God of honour who esteems the humble in heart and lifts up the weak.[2] He despises the proud. He is the one who will judge the living and the dead and we should fear Him over anything else in the world because He is greater than the world. I think if we truly understood the account we will have to give to God one day we would give so much more thought to how we live.

I believe if we understood the awesome responsibility we hold before God we'd tread carefully with more reverence. When faced with the choice to sin or not to sin we'd soberly fear the judgment of God. God holds us accountable for each day, you know. This is an unpopular topic for many because many people want God to conform to their image of Him! They want to see Him like Father Christmas and there's no denying He's abundant in His blessing, mercy and longsuffering of humankind. But if we are to accept God we must accept Him for who HE says He is. He is love but He is also Justice and Truth.

If you have sought Him with a repentant heart, be assured you are loved and under His grace. But one day our future will be to stand before him and give an account of ourselves.[3] That kinda scares the pants off me, I don't know about you. I know I'm going to heaven but I want to take the treasures of a holy life in there with me. On that day God will ask me what I did with the talents He gave me on this earth and as He gazes upon them His eyes of fire will burn away anything that I secretly did for my glory. He will burn away anything which was not undertaken with a pure motivation. I wonder when He's finished if there'll be anything of worth left? I really hope so because I know the inclinations of my own heart and babe at times I know they're not that great.

I want to implore you to develop a healthy fear of the Lord in this journey of life girlfriend, for it will protect you from so much. Proverbs 31 v 30 *"Charm is deceptive and beauty is fleeting; but a woman who fears the Lord is to be praised."*

[1]Prov 9 v 10
[2]Isaiah 66 v 2
[3]1 Peter 4 v 5

Drop 59 ~ Seasons

Life is about seasons. We're hidden within the winter of the womb and brought forth into the fragility of spring growth. We dance and bear fruit throughout the summer and slow down and ultimately return to the warm earth in the autumn. My friend's Dad died recently and she showed me a beautiful photo album which her mum had made up of his life. There was a photo for every year he was upon this earth, he was obviously much loved. I was reflecting about this and how each season in his life was captured in that book. His first steps, his first day at school, his first shirt and tie, his wedding day, his first child and many other events in a happy life. While the album captured moments it could never account for the richness of the detail of each season of this dear man's life.

As children of God we will go through seasons of… equipping, warfare, resting, tactical practice, teaching, discipline, healing… each one being crafted by the one who loves you the most. Be assured He works with such a delicate touch, with such detail and with such love woven right through the tapestry of your life. But He will only do what you allow Him to do. He will not force Himself upon you. Sadly many people struggle through the seasons of their life because they've put a no entry sign on the door of their hearts. If they only knew the healing, the wholeness, the blessing awaiting them on the other side of that door…

God's been teaching me a lot about seasons recently. In each season God is always creating…even in seasons of rest. Whatever season we are in God has shown me the importance of staying put until God has finished the work of that season. If we try to rush on to the next season we will be lacking in development, healing, strength or other essential elements. Ask yourself, how can I work with God as He weaves the rich tapestry of my life? And lastly… don't rush the seasons of your life, because life is over in the blink of an eye. Enjoy, grow and learn from the season you're in…

Prayer… Father I thank you that all the detail of my life is held in your loving hand, woven and purposed into your awesome tapestry. Give me the wisdom and strength to work with you in the joy and the pain of the seasons you have ordained for me. Help me to carry threads of pure gold to invest in the tapestries of others and when my seasons have reached their end, may I have brought a smile to your heart. Amen.

Psalm 1 v 3 " *Girlfriend you are like a tree planted by streams of living water which yields it fruit in season and your leaves do not wither but you will prosper in all you do" - Paraphrased*

Drop 60 ~ Rebel without a cause

Ever have a paddy…with God? Let's be real here girls…we all have! I have had a total stomping of my feet, spitting, kicking screaming, grade 6 on the Richter scale tantrum with the Lord before now. Do you know what's really funny? Rebelling against God is totally fruitless. He is always bigger and stronger and in control when we're not. Unlike us, He is always going to have pure love as His motivation and clear perspective which is outside of time.

Rebellion is simply pride. It says my will and not thine. Looking back at my life when I wanted things my way, I am convinced destruction would have been the fruit had God answered my prayers. It's often only with the luxury of hindsight that we can see God holds out for what will bring us life, where we just want it NOW! I have a friend who once told me God always brings revelation not revolution; isn't that a fact?! Revelation is a revealing of His perfect and good will, revolution, well that's simply destructive not creative…

Rebellion is so subtle it sneaks up on you. Next time you feel rebellious consider the motives behind your feelings. It may be a lack of trust; do you trust God to keep His word? It may be your motive is impatience when His timing is not in keeping with yours. Beloved, nothing will rob your purpose, your calling faster than a rebellious heart. Refuse to allow seeds of rebellion a foothold.

Rebellion happens like this… first you feel a wee niggly feeling, then you'll find every time you hear _blank_ mentioned it's a much bigger niggle. Soon the old critical juices rise up and start bubbling… Mmmm smell that smell… Oh once that's cooking nicely and your pride is rolling along with momentum the superior self starts to voice its opinion *which can only be right because self opinion is always right*! And before you know it… yes actually…! YOUR way is the only way of doing things because you know best. Ouch…!!

I'm laughing to myself as I write this because it's so real, it's what we do. God is so totally gracious when we stand before Him with arms crossed and feet tapping! Let's face it we are flawed and imperfect; can we really know better than the Almighty God who made the vast Heavens? In proverbs it says the plans of a man's heart are many but it's the purposes and plans of God which will prevail.[1] Do you trust your Father who is nuts about you and whose motivation towards you is always love?

Stop wrestling with God because He'll win and you'll waste your energy, time and strength and joy in the process.

[1]Proverbs 19 v 21

1 Samuel 15 v 22-23 *"Does the Lord delight in burnt offerings and sacrifices as much as in obeying the voice of the Lord? To obey is better than sacrifice and to heed God is better than the fat of rams. For rebellion is like the sin of divination and arrogance like the evil of idolatry..."*

Drop 61 ~ <u>It's a brand new day</u>

Every day is brand spanking new, yesterday is gone and we can't have it back. But today… well princess, today awaits you with a new dawn. Do you know each day says, "*Welcome, this is your day, child of God!*"

Today started about four this morning as creation gathered to welcome her in… birds started singing and a glow of light fanned over the horizon, as the stars still twinkled in the sky and the voice of God whispered to your sleeping ear, darling, just for you. As the dew spread its bridal silk over the green grass and the breeze blew through the trees, the voice of God whispered, darling, just for you. The earth warmed as the sun arose and its brilliance reflecting the joy of Heaven and as He watched you sleep, God's smile beamed and He whispered, darling just for you. As you came to the surface from your slumber the unseen excitement of life grew and grew till the moment you opened your eyes. It was then Heaven erupted with joy as you awoke and your God declared, "She's awake!! Welcome, welcome cherished child, welcome to another day…darling this is for you, just for you.

Child, you are the loved beyond measure, princess of the kingdom of Heaven, precious and dearly loved daughter of the Almighty. He has clothed you in royal robes and set a crown upon your head and as you waken each day, sings over you new songs of love. Only sometimes life gets so hassled and busy that we forget who we are. Sometimes sadly we forget who He is and how much He delights in us. Each day is a gift from God (even when it doesn't feel like it); He has blessings, lessons and love stored up especially for you in each day. He is a God of purpose who is passionately interested in every detail of your life. Honey bun, if it matters to you…it matters to God. Every morning is a brand new day with your name it!

I am *sooo* not a morning person but, one of the greatest experiences of my life was getting up to watch the sunrise. I got up about four while it was still dark, wrapped a big blanket around myself, got a hot drink and went to the back garden. It was awesome...! The noise of the bird song was deafening; I never realised how much welly they give it because we've got double glazing. What's amazing is for about ten minutes just before the first beam of day break they all go quiet like they're anticipating the miracle of a new day. As soon as the sun comes up for certain they go bonkers again. PLEASE make the opportunity to do this while you have breath in your body. You won't be disappointed. Well you might if you do it in the rain! Yeah that's a point, wait till you have a nice crisp morning, then enjoy the delights as creation cries out the praise of the creator!

Lamentation 23 v 22-23 *"Because of the Lord's great love we are not consumed, for His compassions never fail. They are new every morning, great is your faithfulness."*

Drop 62 ~ Heaven hears (so does hell)

Don't you just hate whingers? I can't stand them, they totally do my head in and I have to admit my lack of patience comes to the fore in their presence. We've a few at our church, every church does…yeah, you know who you are! I have to confess I try to not even stand near them when its coffee time. Gripe, gripe, gripe… In our house we call them fun suckers! That was 'S' for suckers, tut tut... And this is a Christian book!! *(I just put that in to see how many of them write to the publishers and complain!)* I know, I'm dreadful…anyhow now I've got that off my chest and have fought the urge to slap a few people I'll get on with the crux of the message!

Which is…be careful what you say, because sinning simply comes naturally to us, we've got to make a conscious effort not to do it. It takes practice to look for positive things because negativity is second nature to us. I was listening to a sermon recently and the pastor Deborah Cobre,[1] pointed out that when we speak, Heaven hears and so does Hell. That's why every day we need to ask the Holy Spirit to fill us with him and empty out the dross of our flesh.

Princess, when we speak negatively, Hell hears! Yes, the powers of darkness hear when we put spin on a situation, or whinge about the colour of the loo roll - I think we need to be so careful. I picture demonic agitators are released in our direction and we lay ourselves open to attack when we get all negative. The Bible tells us that grumbling and whinging is what keep the Israelites in the desert for 40 years when their trip should have taken 11 days - EEK! You work out the ratio of wasted time in that!

I have too much I want to do in this life to hold myself back by grumbling and whinging. The other thing that strikes me is that whinging actually keeps you in the place of your frustration. If grumbling kept the Israelites in the desert perhaps grumbling about your husband, your kids, your finances is keeping you in the place of your frustration. Girlfriends, don't give the enemy ammunition to hold you in the bondage of your frustration or the ability to wound because of the sin of whinging…

Next time you come across a fun sucker choose to bless them. See them as a casualty and pray the Lord will give you a way to love them into healing and be gracious to them, for we all come from different places and you don't know the life they've had…. Now where's Mrs So and So…?!

Galatians 5 v 13 *"You my sisters were called to be free, but do not use your freedom to indulge your sinful nature rather serve one another in love."*

[1]Pastor Deborah Cobre – 'Overcoming Offences' Rock Church California 2345 S. Waterman Avenue. San Bernardino, CA 92408

Drop 63 ~ When life shatters in a moment.

"If the whole structure of your existence shattered, like a precious vase onto a stone floor, can the pieces be gathered up and by some re-creative miracle be put together again to be an object of beauty?" [1]

Mmmm ... Have you been there? Are you there now? We can paddle along in life then… wham! An explosion happens that devastates all we thought we knew. Our principles are challenged and the very foundations of our life shaken.

Being brought up in Northern Ireland I experienced my fair share of explosions. I remember being filled with a sense of wonder as the ground shook and your ears popped with the pressure of shock waves. Explosions always seemed to happen when you were doing something really mundane. Like using the loo or washing your Dad's car! When your world falls apart, the timing's always wrong… When everything in your world changes in a moment, what then…?

Can we recover, even grow? I believe we can but it's a slow and often messy process. To use the analogy of decorating a room - when the wallpaper's torn, exposing the rising damp, and there are lumps of plaster all over the place it looks pretty messy, ugly even. When we've been torn apart and what appeared to be fine on the surface is laid bare we will have to go through the restoration process of God's love. When the bits of dead worm-ridden wood have been removed, when we've been treated with preservative and the cracks filled, the result is something much stronger than what was there originally. The same finish or surface can be applied and the wall may look just as it did before, but it's not. Underneath it is restored and stronger. Princess when something has caused pain within the core of your being and you surrender yourself to the loving hand of the Father, you will come through and underneath you will be restored and stronger.

When the shell of normality is taken away and we feel like an exposed jelly, the only place of protection and the beginning of healing is in the embrace of God. In those very times of vulnerability God works deeply in the character of our souls if we allow Him. If we rest under the shadow of His wing and dare to trust in the unseen God and His promises, He will give us peace and assurance in an uncertain world. That peace may feel a bit wobbly at first but persevere, there is peace there.

If you are sitting in a broken world, if your reality has exploded and the shock waves are still trembling please know, Our God never changes, He is ALWAYS good and He ALWAYS cares more than my mere words could ever express. Know, just like that precious vase, not only will you be more beautiful but you will be stronger.

Psalm 34 v 18 *"The Lord is close to the broken hearted, and saves those who are crushed in spirit."*

[1]"Rebuilding Your Broken World" By Gordon MacDonald – 1988 , pg.10, foreword by Vernon Grounds: Nelson USA

Drop 64 ~ Never ending story

It's amazing how our senses can influence us with such strength. We can smell some aftershave or perfume and instantly we're transported to a certain place and time in memory. There was a song on the radio the other day 'Never Ending Story' which was a big hit in the 80's and it just made me feel cheerful. While I can't remember what events were taking place in my world at that time I just know this song triggered in me a happy feeling, Yippee...! So...yes, is there a point? Well let's see...I was thinking why I liked that song, most of the words are nonsense. But this idea of a never-ending story got my juices bubbling. You see life is quite simply a never-ending story. There is always something more, something unseen. This is not it....!

As Christians we believe that there is a bigger picture, there is more to this life than meets the eye. I praise God that the here and now is temporary, that we do have hope, that in the midst of uncertainties we can fix our eyes on the one thing that is pure and true, Jesus Christ. 2 Corinthians 4 v 16 -18: "Therefore do not lose heart. Though outwardly we are wasting away, yet inwardly we are being renewed day by day; for our light and momentary troubles are achieving for us an eternal glory that far outweighs them all. So we fix our eyes not on what is seen, but what is unseen. For what is seen is temporary, but what is unseen is eternal."

By focusing on the fact that this life is simply the dress rehearsal for the never ending story of our eternal lives we can take comfort when the here and now is tough. I pray today you'll be touched by the exciting life which awaits you in eternity where we'll have never ending joy. I'm also burdened by the hope that you may need for the troubles or the heartache of today; and the better thing is God is concerned with that too. He wants you to overcome, to be happy and have mad moments of fun!

Is there a c.d. or song that makes you feel happy? It doesn't have to be Christian, just one. Go and put it on really loud and dance round your kitchen or anywhere you have a space. *(NB. This is usually easier to do when you have the house to yourself!)* I do that all the time and promise it will lift your spirits. It may also remind you that it's good to lose your inhibitions once in a while! YAHOO....!

Psalm 149 v 3 *"Let them praise His name with dancing and make music to Him with tambourine and harp."*

Drop 65 ~ Grab hold of yer fundamentals!

Ok so you have said the 'sinner's prayer' and go to church, you may even read books other than the psalms… BUT what do you (one on one) actually believe? It's really easy to get confused in this world as we are bombarded with so much stuff everyday, and that's just information. On top of that there's negotiating all the relationship dilemmas we can find ourselves in. You know the ones where you wonder if you can tell your good friend she has broccoli in her teeth. A few years ago a government slogan in Britain was 'getting back to basics', yeah …catchy! Anyway what are the simple profound basic fundamental truths in your relationship with God? Do you know you are cherished? Do you know you can trust? What about God's grace to you, do you know you're forgiven for yesterday and tomorrow?

Sometimes when other faith followers quiz me about mine I find it a real source of certainty to go back to what I simply know. For me that is that God loves me and He answers prayer. Everything else in my life stems from those two truths. When life is rubbish and I'm walking through a tough time, I grab hold of the fundamental (God loves me). When I wake up as I sometimes do and wonder if God is something I just want to believe in, I grab hold of the fundamental (He has answered again and again my prayers in miraculous ways) and this causes my faith to burst out all over the place.

It's good to grab hold of your fundamentals just to refresh your memory about the certainty of what you've chosen to base your life on. John Ortberg, one of my favourite writers defines these crux building blocks as foundational truths. Some of his are …

- God is always present and active in my life whether I see him or not.
- My task is to meet God in this moment.
- Whenever I fail I can always start again in a new moment.
- My desire for God ebbs and flow, but He desires me constantly.
- The way I experience God is unique to me.*

And my favourite…

- How I process every thought matters. It carries a spiritual charge that moves me a little closer or a little further from God.

John 14 v 6 *"I am the way, the truth and the life. No-one comes to the Father except through me."*

*God is closer than you think. pg.25, John Ortberg. Zondervan USA, 2005.

Drop 66 ~ The boomerang effect!

Throw the thing away and YEP! It comes back to you… How many times have I prayed to the Lord and given Him the burden only to find a wee while after I'm carrying the same thing back to Him again in prayer? Yeah all the preachers tell us to trust every worry to the Lord and that's totally right…But… How practically can you do this? Is there a method or a technique to doing this because I've found it very difficult? Well… I'm not sure if I can give you a methodology, sweet cheeks, but I can tell you what's worked for me…

1) Identify the *real* root of the upset – perhaps you're actually frustrated, angry, rebellious or scared or whatever (this takes humility and time to wait on the Holy Spirit to reveal the truth).

2) Once you've identified the root and before you 'do' anything, surrender the outcome of the upset to God – totally! This really has maximum power when verbalising this out loud. So you might say something like, "*Lord I give the outcome of - this money worry, job worry, whatever worry… to you. Father however this plays out I surrender completely to your will. If it goes how I want it to, Praise you; if it goes differently I will still choose to Praise you.*"

3) If there's something practical you know you need to do, get on and do it, don't arse about dithering; that'll just add to your stress!

4) Start praising - best done out loud babe! Declare the truth of God! This might go something like, "*Lord you are my rock, my faithful friend and I choose to praise you, and I lift the name of Jesus up in praise because the Name of Jesus is all powerful. Your word tells me to submit to you in order that I may have the power to resist the devil so he and any distress to me will flee. Praise you Lord that I am more than a conqueror in the mighty name of Jesus, Praise you Father that you care about me in this situation and will work all things to grow and educate me for your glory and my good….*"

5) You may feel a temporary relief but here's the thing, you've gotta dodge the boomerang on the way back. As sure as anything 5 mins after you stop praying the same boomerang will try and make its way back to you again. This is the crucial bit of my tactic… verbally say something like, *"I refuse to*

think about this issue any further because I have given it to God and He is trustworthy."

Dodging boomerangs takes a bit of practice. I have found God developing this reflex in my spirit. So many times, worry tries to engage me in debate with myself again. So many times I have to literally STOP – SURRENDER – PRAISE and refuse to get drawn into mulling… I still get the odd whack to the side of the head but I'm getting better!

*Practical point, you may find it helpful to jot down burdens, give them to God in prayer, then bin or burn the bit of paper.

1 Peter 5 v 7 *"Cast all your cares upon Him for He cares for you."*

Drop 67 ~ Ah… that's better

I have just had a wonderful half hour curled up on the sofa with a hot chocolate and a glossy mag and no distractions… ah heaven! Oh isn't it good to take time and simply… be? I wonder how often do we practise the discipline of an unhurried life? I know some of you reading this are juggling so many plates and the thought of just being still for 5 seems like a nasty joke but please don't throw this book at the wall till you've heard me out!

We all have differing amounts of money, energy, friends or any other number of things; but all of us will only ever have 24hrs in the day. No more, no less. I see people all the time who cram their lives so full of stuff that they quite literally don't have time to think. Perhaps it is a way of avoiding pain or dealing with deep issues too horrendous to unpack, or perhaps it's just following the herd? I really do believe that being too busy is sinful. To be so busy that you're unthinking is not living in the fullness of Christ and to the glory of God. When we're too busy nothing ever gets done right, it gets what my mother would call a lick and a promise. The very real danger is we develop a 'that'll do' attitude particularly to the things that scream the least for our attention. We develop a reactive fire fighting response rather than a proactive choice. This breeds frustration because things don't ever then get done as well as we know they could be.

Too often key relationships in our lives come last on our list when we're running just to stand still! Princess, Jesus never hurried. He always took His time and the most time He took was for prayer and people. Gosh sometimes life really isn't rocket science, eh? When it comes to the crunch what really matters - when the pretense of life is cut away and you are staring into eternity, what will matter? It's not your big TV, or new car. It's very simply 1st God and 2nd people. In fact in Exodus 20 God tells us much the same thing – put me first then each other.

Today so much of life happens within our microwave mentality. Speed dating, pop tarts, instant internet access and Velcro help speed up our lives (n*ot that I'm knocking any of those)*. However, where there is an impatient mentality driving life it becomes another form of enslavement as we are driven and not led. Have you ever have found yourself getting unreasonably angry when you feel your time has been wasted? Or rushing through life at a million MPH with no head space? If you do princess I fear you might have microwave sickness. Microwave sickness will rob your very life of meaning so it's serious stuff honey bun! Your love for other people will disappear as you hurry from point to point with a false sense of accomplishment. But thankfully there is a treatment.

Next time you feel frustration rising, or can't remember when you last enjoyed life, try this treatment…

- Step one – Jesus took time to pray and to love. (*How's your prayer life going? When did you last wait on God and allow Him to fill you with His approval, confidence and love?)*
- Step two - take a deep breath and think of 5 things in your life to be thankful for. (*Happy fulfilled people have learned the art of gratitude and culture the habit of a thankful heart.)*
- Step three - consciously slow down. Try chewing your food, walking instead of taking the car. Budget more time for tasks, learn people will still like you if you say 'no' and if you find you've time spare, go back and redo the above!

Girlfriend let us discipline our pace, let us mellow like a good wine as we journey through life. We don't get to go back and redo this thing; life is what you carve out for yourself. So slow down and make it beautiful, beautiful, you deserve it!

Psalm 46 v 10 *"Be still and know that I am God…"*

Drop 68 ~ String theory

Psalm 33 v 2 *"Praise the Lord with the harp; make music to Him with the ten stringed lyre."*

I watched a bit of a documentary about Steven Hawkins the other night, I say a bit because most of the physics stuff is way over my head. Anyway the gist of my understanding was that this guy was in the process of a theory to explain everything... The confusing thing was that as the theory outworked it seemed to throw up more questions than it actually answered! Anyway the whole string theory got me thinking because the more I look into science the more I see the hand of my God.

God has not created confused random matter, just look at the solar system! Listen to the harmony of bird song or think about the joy of friendship; no honey bun, there is a method in God's madness for sure. I love the wonder of music which has been shown scientifically to aid healing and soothe the soul. My husband plays the guitar and he's teaching our wee son. It's so cute to see them together...awww... anyway, I was thinking about the strings of the guitar. You know in a way they are just like us...

It's only when a string is stretched the sound is tuned. Mmm... are you seeing the parallels? Perhaps it is when we are stretched in the flesh we are being tuned into Heaven's perfect pitch. Thinking about the churches in our nation I wonder how tuned are its instruments? Are we really stretching, straining towards the prize, tuned and ready for playing pleasure; or are we slack stringed, woeful sounding and well... ineffective. I have thought about times in my own life where I have sacrificed the pursuit of God's agenda to my own slack and lazy attitude.

When a church in unity is being stretched it is possible to rejoice because the tuning of Heaven's song is happening in the process, each string being tuned to harmonise and make a beautiful sound with the others. I believe this is the call of the bridegroom to His church. He desperately wants us to stretch towards unity for His glory in line with His word; both in our individual lives and corporately as His bride.

Sweetie pie you can trust the master musician to tune you with His gentle accuracy, ensuring the tension for your own perfect pitch, your unique elongation process which, when undertaken in *HIS* way, will never cause you to snap. Please know that even though you may feel uncomfortable and stretched at times you are producing sweet music of eternity.

Are there tensions in your world right now…? Go and cuddle up with the one who can fine tune any circumstance to your good and His glory!

Isaiah 42 v 3 *"A bruised reed He will not break and a smouldering wick He will not snuff out. In faithfulness He will bring forth justice."*

Drop 69 ~ I need a hero!

So often Jesus is pictured as this insipid white wimpy boy, but let's face it, Jesus Christ was born in the Middle East. He didn't have blonde hair and blues eyes! He worked hard in a physically demanding job, so He was probably quite butch and He hung out with the guys. He didn't lie around on clouds stroking bunnies, lisping His way through woosy parables and smiling inanely as He sprinkled life with rose petals…somebody bring me a bucket!

Sometimes life can feel very overwhelming and unfair, it's in those moments I need to know I am loved by an action man, not a big girl's blouse. How about you? Do you know the one who protects you is a true knight in shining armour, the hero who'll beat up the baddies and save the object of His affection, you His princess? Do you know your prayers are heard by Heaven's champion and all hell fears that it's messed with a child of the living God when you claim your heritage in prayer? You are the beloved of the real and only action hero…

Life is unjust at times and maybe you've been dreadfully hurt and betrayed in the past. Perhaps playground taunts grew to shape your adulthood or your trust and love have been cheapened and rejected. But I want to offer you this hope for all those circumstances which wounded you. You Princess _________ are loved so much that your Hero gave His life so you might live; the really cool part is that this hero cannot die. He has overcome death and so all hell knows the time of reckoning grows shorter and shorter. The time is coming when every demonic power which manipulated situations in your life to cause hurt will have to stand before your lover, your protector and pay the price of justice. That scares the life out of hell I can assure you. The wrath of God is not something to underestimate! It's tempting to look to other people at times for protection but I've learned ONLY He can bring true deliverance and peace. Do you need peace or deliverance in a situation in your world today?

Know God hears your prayers so just hang on, your hero your knight in shining armour will come, riding on a white horse to save the day… His timing is perfect; be expectant in prayer and trust this promise of God!

Revelation 19 v 11-13 tells it like this…. *"Then I saw Heaven open wide – and there before me was a white horse whose rider was named faithful and true. With justice He judges and makes war. His eyes are like blazing fire, and on His head are many crowns. He has a name written on Him that no one else knows but himself. He is dressed in a robe dipped in blood and His name is The Word of God."*

If you're feeling like you need reminding of the awesome power of your God go start from 19 v 11 and read on through the rest of Revelation.

Drop 70 ~ Cost of the call

Mmmm… there's nothing like the smell of fresh coffee, I know people who don't even like coffee but like the smell! Good coffee costs a bit extra but it's worth the price. Coffee, picked by people who are given dignity and a fair price, roasted and served up is such a blessing, oh my… I might have to put the kettle on before I write any more! Ok to sort of wander *to* the point, coffee is a bit like the call on each of our lives when we respond to the hope of salvation. I realise by this stage of this book you're a very tolerant person and will hang on in there reading in the hope I'll have a point! And I actually do babe honest…

Good coffee is authentic and costs, yep that's my point. You can get freeze dried coffee, flavoured coffee, even Soya substitute coffee, but it's not the same as the real thing. We can live with a second rate standard of purpose, our packaging can be very trendy but it's the flavour, the smell the colour of our walk that will distinguish us as authentic top notch stuff. A friend of mine told me a story recently about a coffee bean; when it's dropped in hot water, rather than dissolve it changes the very water its dropped in… into something wonderful…Coffee!

The cost of loving Jesus can leave us feeling like we're in hot water and great discomfort at times. But girlfriend, it's in those times that we can choose how we respond to the heat and either dissolve or fragrance. There will be times you've got to swallow your anger, frustration, pride or whatever… and pray with passion for a quick blast of graciousness! There will be things that you have longed for which you'll have to surrender in order to follow God's way over your own. You know that's really hard… really, really hard. I know in my life when I've had to pay big time for my obedience to God's will over my own I have always grown as a result. I can honestly say my God has never short changed me when I've chosen to fragrance rather than dissolve.

There have been many, many times I've been more of a sugar lump than coffee bean and my wonderful God gets that; but the point is, just keep trying. The cost is worth the wonderful result not only for you, but all those people in your world whose lives you fragrance each day. Be bold, be strong, for the lord your God is with you!

2 Corinthians 2 v 15 - *"For we are to God the aroma of Christ among those who are being saved and those who are perishing."*

Drop 71 ~ History maker… moi?

I was cleaning congealed strawberry yogurt off the side of the bin the other night; yeah my life is a dizzy world of champagne, lights, sequins, and glamour, not…! Anyway, as I did I wondered if awesome people like Mother Teresa or Hudson Taylor knew they were changing the course of history. I think not. I think they were just getting on with the job the Lord had put into their hands at the time; faithfully, dutifully, obediently and humbly getting on with it. I don't think their jobs in life were any more interesting or less messy than cleaning the floor, but they carried out their duties with diligence and commitment.

I wonder, when Mother Teresa cleaned the sores of a leper if she realised just how God would use her to model His love to the world? I wonder if Hudson Taylor when he knelt down to pray knew he would model to a whole generation the faithfulness of God's provision through prayer. When William Wilberforce campaigned against slavery or Corrie Ten Boom modelled forgiveness in Jewish concentration camps, these people, albeit painfully and at great cost, were simply allowing the character of Christ to shine in the frailty of who they were.

I passionately want to be a useful child to my heavenly Father and bear fruit. But here's the thing, God has put work, yes humble work into my hands right now and I truly believe I'm just as effective mopping a floor to His glory as I am changing the world. There's a story about a young Oxford graduate who went to a Buddhist monastery for a year. This guy had been top of his class and had many accomplishments under his belt for a young man. His first job in the monastery was to clean the toilets. Upon hearing this he became very indignant and said to the head monk "Do you know who I am and what I have accomplished." The lama said "Yes great things I know you can do but the little things I have yet to see."

Honey bun, don't despise the little things, they are building the stuff of character into you.

Are you plodding through life, juggling 101 different roles? If so I want to encourage you today to be extraordinary in the ordinariness of your life. I want to encourage you to make that speech, fill in those forms, help with that project, wipe that bum and do it all to the glory of God. You can shape the history of tomorrow by what you do in the ordinariness of today. You go girl….!

1 Corinthians 10 v 31 *"Whatever you do, do it all to the Glory of God the Father in Heaven"*

Go 'Google' some of the above people and be inspired… they thought they were no one special but, Wow what a shape they left in history!

Drop 72 ~ Diamond in the rough

Have you seen you Disney film 'Aladdin'? At the beginning there is a scene where an unworthy person tries to steal part of the secrete treasure. Upon failing they are told to seek out a diamond in the rough. I love this expression because it sums up something of value which appears very ordinary at first glance. Did you know you're a diamond to the Lord? You are of very precious worth and value.

Consider the attributes of a diamond… They take a long time to form. It is no quick process, it takes time. The process of becoming a diamond doesn't happen in a very pleasant place. It's dark, damp and hard. It's only by extreme pressure of weight bearing down on top of the piece of coal that the impurities are squeezed out rendering the coal to perfection and strength. Diamonds don't look like much in the dirt and rocks in which they are formed. In order for a diamond's worth to be uncovered the skill of a master craftsman is required. Once cut there is no stronger blade or precision instrument than a diamond, they can engrave and leave a mark on anything.

So what has any of that got to do with me, I hear you cry…?!
Well sweet cheeks, I believe we are all diamonds in the rough. It takes a lifetime for us to form, but that formation happens in the secret place one on one with God. **The deepest most valuable times of your life seldom have an audience.** It's tough when life presses upon us, when loneliness and darkness seem to be all we feel. But we are never alone, He is with us and is at work for the greater good. It's painful as we allow the process of God's purification to squeeze out the things which would seek to hold us to a lesser value.

Sin always wants a less than < direction for your life, God always wants more than > direction for you. Girlfriends don't settle for being a lump of coal - you're a diamond in the rough! It hurts when others only see you as a dirty lump of worthless rock. God knows the pain of being underestimated and devalued everyday. Yet He knows His worth and what's more He knows yours! And finally it takes Jesus to mine us out from the dirt where we are at, wash us and present us to the master craftsman the Father God.

In His skilled hands we can be shaved and shaped into so much more than we appear both to ourselves and others. In His hands we can be used to etch our mark for His glory upon eternity's history. I praise God I'm a diamond in the rough, don't you?

Philippians 1 v 6 *"Be confident of this, He who began a good work in you will carry it on to completion until the day of Christ Jesus."*

Drop 73 ~ Real love

The simple truth about love is that it's a choice. It comes with no guarantee and no strings; it stands alone, an act of free will. Wow how different is that definition from what the world puts forwards as love? Because He loved the world, Christ chose the cross. Because Christ loved us, He chose us. Because He loves, He chooses not to give up on us in our wobbly moments, He chose to demonstrate His love with no assurance we'd even respond to His call two thousand years down the line.

When God met me in the mess I'd made of my life, I really did experience His cleansing power and restorative healing. This was a process which took time and discipline. In His love He gave me back dignity which had been dreadfully eroded and new hope. He wooed me and spoke tender words of love to me in my darkest hours and, weird as it sounds, I fell head over heels in love with this invisible hero. Girlfriend, just as birds were created to fly, we were created to give and to receive love. Jesus really does want to be your love object because beloved, you are His.

Real love is Jesus shaped… you can trust him to fill the voids in your soul. There are areas within each of us which are never totally satisfied because we've not allowed Christ to meet the desire there. Instead we've settled for a superficial and temporary love fix. With Jesus you really can fall totally in love. He's totally trustworthy, and totally different from any other person you'll ever love. Like many of you I've been fractured by broken promises and empty words but I can honestly say with Jesus it is very different…

In the first year of falling in love with Jesus it was exciting, a bit like human love only less predictable with more discovering. Over the course of time, my love for Him has become more like a long term relationship with a more committed type of love coupled with a huge sense of trust. This is great but the danger is that we become as the song says "accustomed to His face". There are times when love for God will cool, there will be times you feel disillusioned and wonder if you've backed the wrong horse. Hunny bun, this is NORMAL! I understand what it feels like to have invested your whole heart into a relationship with an invisible hero only to wonder if he's walked out on you too! There are times when the Lord will seem very far away and you'll wonder if He hears or even cares? It says in Hosea[1] the Lord at times takes you to a desert place. Why would He do that, why would He want you to suffer the heat, the thirst or the barrenness if He loved you?

He longs to woo your cool heart…His passion unlike ours, never fades but we are fickle and ours does. So often we limit God in our minds; when life is not going to plan we assume God changes. Beloved God is always GOOD, He never changes but we do. So He wants to mature your love, your faith. I've learned that when I'm in a desert place I have a choice to make. Will I trust God in that quiet place or will I bail? You see, love makes the choice to stay committed despite our own feelings of emptiness.

Sometimes we need to ignore the doubts which will bombard us from every angle and catch our deepest most private vulnerabilities. It is in these times of incommunicado that God is looking at you with eyes of love, willing you to choose commitment over feeling. This is grown up love, girlfriend. Sometimes He needs to step back so we can get out of the rut, wake up and rediscover the fondness of an absent heart. I want to encourage you if you are in a desert place today…

You will not die… despite how you feel. Exercise grown up love, choose your response, commit in your emptiness and He will fill you in His time. In His abounding love you will learn a new appreciation for simple life-giving things like water. You will learn new levels of trust as you realise your utter dependence on your guide outta the mess of life. And precious sister, when you come through you'll have a new love song on your lips.

[1]Hosea 2 v 14 & 15 (The Message)

"And now here's what I'm going to do: I'm going to start all over again. I'm taking her back out into the wilderness where we had our first date, and I'll court her. I'll give her bouquets of roses. I'll turn heart break valley into acres of hope. She'll respond like she did as a young girl, those days when she was fresh out of Egypt."

Drop 74 ~ Don't hold back

People will always have issues. It is part of our human condition! As you run this race you may meet people or situations which question and judge your motives. Girlfriend when you meet other saints with 'issues' you need to know you are programmed for success not failure. In Christ we have the victory over all that would seek to hinder and hold us back. If you find that you are continually put down and criticised, there are some things you must do to gain the glorifying victory which is your birthright.

Firstly and most practically you need to examine yourself before God with a humble heart in prayer: *they may have a point!* In your time of prayer God may reveal things or other perspectives you were unaware of. Secondly press hard into God, pray and pray then pray some more for the person who is seeking to hold you back. And thirdly leave their outcome to the Lord to deal with in His way and in His time. Princess, you simply can't be the answer in that person's life, only Jesus can, so keep walking in love pointing to Him as their solution and keep your beautiful booty moving. In the meantime get on with what the Lord has placed in your hand, keeping love as your motivation for all you do and say.

Babe, we've got to ruthlessly allow nothing, but nothing to hold us back from digging deeper into the rock of our salvation. There may be adjustments we have to make as we negotiate life for His glory but the most important thing you will ever do is draw near to God. Getting closer to God is the priority of every day and glorifying Him is the fruit of your purpose.

Bottom line is we need to be the catalyst for our own vision… if we don't make it happen then who's going to? Girlfriend be inspired by your own sense of purpose, your dreams are valid and wonderful. When we get excited about our destiny we inspire others in theirs. Much in life will seek to hold you back but you can do more than you think… Surrender you plans to your Father who loves you then go for it…. Jump – the world is waiting for you…

You Go Girl, you're awesome!

Hebrews 12 v 1- 2 *"Let us throw off everything that hinders and the sin that so easily entangles, and let us run with perseverance the race marked out for US. Let us fix our eyes on Jesus, the author and perfecter of our faith."*

Drop 75 ~ Gate crashing girl

There's this really cool story in the Bible about a woman called Esther. Make time to read it (it's in the Old Testament), it is gob-smacking the way God works all things for good for those who love Him.... Anyho' the wee bit I wanna focus on is where Esther is queen and all is tickety boo.[1] Every morning her loving uncle Mordecai would go along to the palace gate. In those times the 'gate' was the place where all the wise men and court officials would congregate and discuss matters, a bit like a mini House of Commons or Senate.

Anyway I was thinking about this gate-waiting lark and the Lord dropped into my heart that if I want Him to communicate with me I need to place myself around His gate. If you read the story you'll know Esther would send Mordecai little gifts, send him little communications. We're no different; if we want to communicate with God we've got to wait on Him and long for Him. By waiting in the right place Mordecai was not only blessed, he was strategically placed to hear various perhaps important conversations. He positioned himself in such a way that he received blessing, wisdom and direction.

It's good to check our position, from time to time, are we in a place where we are best placed to hear from God, are we waiting at His gate daily? Are we looking at world events and considering them in relation to His word? You see, honey bun, just by positioning himself in the right place every day, Mordecai was used to save an entire nation. Girlfriend this is sooo exciting...who knows what God is going to do through you in your time? God isn't looking for Rock star Christians who have big personalities (while that's cool too), God is looking for individuals to position themselves near His gate, ready and willing to do the little jobs He gives them to do. Very ordinary people can accomplish great things by simply walking close to the master – Jesus! Just position yourself in the right place everyday and God will work out the time frame of awesome events in your life.

Jeremiah 29 v 11-13 *"For I know the plans I have for you, declares the Lord, plans to prosper you and not harm you, plans to give you a hope and a future. Then you will call upon me and come and pray to me, and I will listen to you. You will seek me and find me when you seek me with* <u>*all*</u> *your heart."*

[1] Esther ch 2 all of it

Drop 76 ~ Fine art, mighty fine

Soren Kierkegaard "Now with God's help I shall become myself."

Perhaps it's my British-ness but sometimes I find I can act 'on my best behaviour' in public and the real me, warts and all, in private. There's nothing wrong with the real me, in fact it may be even nicer than the public me only it's not just so 'managed'. We all have aspects of ugliness in our personalities and try to manage these areas so that the overspill is kept to a minimum. Much of society is governed by these unspoken social rules and expectations, kinda like an unspoken code. It's probably pride or fear or something but the truth is...we are works in progress; we are continually being refined and polished to be more like Jesus. And we simply need to accept who we are.

You are an amazing piece of God's workmanship, His work of art! You see princess... one day sin entered the world and these beautiful works made in the image and likeness of God got vandalized... and so it's continued... Sadly some were damaged more than others. The image of God in us was torn and dirtied, it was burned and over time misshapen and warped. I wonder how you would feel if someone damaged your creation? You would take action and God did... He sent Jesus to be the vehicle of our healing and restoration. So if at times, like me, you get frustrated with aspects of who you are, stop and remind yourself you are being worked on right at this moment. What an awesome thought!

We are immortal spirits living in a mortal world... God gets that! He understands our frustration when money, energy or time limits all we want to do. He empathises when we get it wrong or make mistakes and He forgives when we choose to destroy rather than create. When the messy aspects of our character spill out, He is there to give us hope and perhaps a mop and bucket!! With God there is always a way to restore; it may be that we choose to bring love, life, hope, encouragement into those we do life with and help the creator in the restoration process. Let's not aid the destroyer in *his* process of vandalizing and destruction. *Beloved precious child of God*...let's choose to accommodate the master sculptor in His creation process of mankind.

You are beautiful, you are a work of art... now go and look at your neighbours, co-workers, friends; can you see how amazing they are too?

C.S. Lewis says, "There are no ordinary people - you have never talked to a mere mortal. Nations, cultures, arts, civilizations…these are mortal and their life is to ours as the life of a gnat. But it is immortals we joke with, we marry, we love, we snub and exploit."

Genesis 1 v 27 *"So God created man in His own image, in the image of God He created them, male and female He created them."*

77 ~ You're sooo enjoyable

Did you know you bring joy to your Father in heaven? You don't have to 'do' anything to be enjoyed, you simply are. God looks at you and is captivated by the way you brush your teeth or wally about with your friends. He calls His angels to watch your antics as you walk through life trying so hard to please or be good…and, yeah, at times still mess it up. He sees your human ability to hug and hold, to wince or wander and He loves watching you work it all out. You see girlfriend God isn't like us, He never gets impatient, He never gets frustrated, He is God and without sin and so He can enjoy the perspective of delighting in each one of us as we will be, not as we are.

It's easy to get caught up in the doing of life and see goals or achievement from our human perspective. When I get a project finished I do get a sense of satisfaction and achievement and that's good. It's good to feel like we're making progress, but I'm aware that it's easy to tick the box marked job done and rush on to the next thing without really savouring the enjoyment that we've given God. Psychologists say it takes you to rehearse a simple thing about 200 times in order for it to become automatic, and even then it still needs to be rehearsed in order for the skill to remain. Well, I've started doing something new within this whole idea of God's enjoyment.

When I've reached the end of a task, like writing a report, leading worship or getting the garden done! I'm trying to cultivate the habit of enjoying the moment. You see, God enjoys me, and YOU! His word says He delights in us. So I reckon it's good to stop and take a moment to enjoy the enjoyment of God. To share in the flow of delight from the throne room of heaven and smile back at your loving Father and just bask in the wonder of His enjoyment of you as you triumph and muddle through life!

Psalm 18 v 19 *"The Lord brought me into a spacious place; He rescued me because He delighted in me."*

Psalm 43 v 4 *"Then I will go to the altar of my Father, to God, my joy and my delight. I will praise you with the harp, O God, my God."*

Drop 78 ~ The anaesthetic of denial

How often have I dug my heels in, done it my way and run headlong into a brick wall?! Anyone with me here? In our pride we think, Nah… we can handle the risk, don't we? Oh honey bun if you only knew the brick walls I've hit and the situations I've got myself into because I've done what I've wanted and sipped the poisoned chalice of denial. The first taste is sweet but gosh does it turn bitter in the stomach. Denial is like a drug which soothes our common sense, or God-given consciousness and allows us to drift into irrational complacency about the consequences of our actions. Once we've hung out in the denial zone for a while something dark and powerful starts to happen…

Deception... Deception is a deeper level of anaesthetic, it doesn't make you dopey like the local anaesthetic of denial, no, deception causes unconsciousness to your conscience. When we enter in to the zombie zone of a deceived state we are rendered totally blind to truth… In fact you could argue that when you don't have the truth you no longer have the direction or the life![1] In psychology the type of lie perceived as absolute truth is termed a false construction of reality. You see if we tell ourselves something often enough we will start to believe it. So if I tell myself it's totally fine to judge my work colleague or fantasize about the hot new postman I will soon start to believe that it's ok, when it's sooo not.[2] When we walk in deception, we lay out the welcome mat for destruction! And destruction is a sure thing once you're in deception, believe me it's a scary thing!

To protect against deception ask yourself this, are the choices I make in line with the truth of God's word? If so, cool…. But just so we're clear let me give you a real practical example… say there's a website, a habit or a behaviour you feel the need to justify in order to partake. Stop and consider: the very fact that you're trying to justify why it's ok makes it not ok. See it as a warning light! Bottom line… most of the time we know deep down when something is ok or not. Don't allow the voice of denial to win over the quiet voice of the conscience.

Give yourself the safety net of having a mentor or an older person in the faith in whom you can trust and talk any ambiguities through. Get over any embarrassment you may have about approaching them, we've all denied and been deceived! Save yourself from the bitter pain of regret and the humiliation of denial, make space to think about and measure your choices today. Your life depends on it, princess!

[1]John 14 v 15-17 "*If you love me you will obey what I command. And I will send you another counsellor to be with you for ever – the Spirit of truth. The world cannot accept him, because it neither sees Him nor knows Him. But you know Him, for He lives with you and will be in you.*"

[2] Proverbs 4 v 21 "*For a man's ways are in full view of the Lord, and he examines all his paths.*"

Drop 79 ~ Positive focus

I've got a big nose, a huge shonk, I got it from my father, bless him! I used to think that perhaps I got carried around by the nose as a baby, but no I've just got a big one…! Anyway, by the time I was a teenager I hated my nose so much; every time I looked in the mirror all I'd see was the nose… The first thing I looked at when I met someone for the first time was their lovely small nose. Here's the thing, the more I compared my 'imperfection', the more I focused on it, and the more I lost focus of the positive things about me.

For example I have nice hair which I often get compliments on (when people don't get distracted by the nose!) and I need to focus on that and not the shonk. Let's face it, who of us doesn't have one wee area she doesn't like about herself? I bet if someone asks you to name some things about yourself you dislike you'd be able to reel off a list, but if you were asked to list the things you really like about yourself, would these things so easily come to mind?

We've all got areas of imperfection, accept them but don't focus on them. If we're going to be powerful women we need to focus on our strengths and not our weaknesses. If I thought about how lousy I am at saying no or how rubbish my attitude is at times, I'd never get out of bed for Jesus. I suspect God in His wisdom, knowing how prideful we are, works life so we are dependent on Him rather than our own natural abilities. The other side of this coin however is the importance of walking in truth and learning to celebrate the gifts, noses and all, that He's placed in each one of us.

Perhaps as Christians, we're conditioned to being lowly, humble, self-effacing and not prideful. But false pride gets right up God's nose! I have a beautiful Swedish friend who is totally humble, but when complimented on a job well done will agree because it's the truth! Go and make a list of ten things that are good about **YOU** then praise your Father who put them there…

Song of Songs 1 v 15 *"How beautiful you are, my darling! Oh how beautiful! Your eyes are like doves."*

P.S. I have embraced the shonk and am actually ok with my nose these days!

Drop 80 ~ God – Credit

Psalm 116 v 12 "*How can I repay the Lord for all His goodness towards me?*"

It's totally ironic being a follower of Jesus at times. He died for us, made a way out of the mess of this world through to a glorious eternal life. We owe Him everything, because if we died tomorrow it would not be the end of the story. Yahoo..! However, and here's the irony, at times it can seem like God isn't keeping His side of the bargain - like giving us freedom, strength, peace, love, protection and all the other promises. It's been an area we all struggle in at times. Girlfriend, it's hard to sing songs like 'Peace like a river' or 'Joy like a fountain' when this is not the reality of your experience, isn't it? In fact it can seem to reinforce a sense of isolation as you stand in church when everyone else is happy-clappy!

This journey really is filled with ups and downs, beliefs and, yes, doubts too… But here's what I know… I know God loves us and gets us better than we 'get' ourselves. I know God doesn't lie and I know His motive towards me (and you) is always love. There will be time when we're leading the happiness and the clappiness, Praise God!! But there will be times of lament and struggle too and sometimes it's useful to understand this is also part of the journey. I was talking about aspects of struggles with a genuinely holy woman and she said, "Sometimes we just need to give God a loan, God sometimes needs to owe us our explanation on the other side of eternity, because of the dynamics of a situation." Could you lend God an extension of patience, faith or even belief?" Flip, imagine God needing me or you to owe Him anything?

You see God's ways are known only to Him and He knows what he needs to accomplish and while you feature in His plans, sometimes He may need you to be less demanding and cut Him some gracious slack! Beloved, His timing is perfect and forged in love. I wonder, if we truly realised how much graciousness and generosity of heart was extended to us, how much more we'd extend it to God. After all, He owes us nothing!

When someone you love asks you to sacrifice something for them or give them credit, it's ok, because you love them and disregard the cost. Next time you're all outta hope and God still hasn't answered those tear filled prayers and belief is faltering…it may help to remember that God loves you and He sees the big picture and abundant grace to carry you through tough times is there for the taking… just ask, princess!

Isaiah 55 v 8 & 9 "*For my thoughts are not your thoughts, neither are your ways my ways, declares the Lord. As the heavens are higher than the earth so are my ways higher than your ways and my thoughts than your thoughts.*"

Drop 81 ~ Be prepared

I have a friend who once, in her rush out of the house to catch her bus, forgot to put her bra on! I sadly could never forget to put a bra on… I think I'd notice as my boobs bounced off my knees (breast-feeding has much to answer for!). But flip, wouldn't you die of embarrassment! Anyway I know many people who spend their lives in a frazzle, rushing round and kind of reacting to life. But here's the thing, life shouldn't actually be chaotic; it should be full and fruit-filled, full of ups and downs, but not chaotic. When we're frazzled we make really bad decisions and live in stress which isn't good for us. When we are 'reacting' rather than making proactive choices, life is pretty exhausting. We don't have a sense of achievement and purpose because we're not actually accomplishing much. Chaos keeps us on a treadmill of unproductive-ness and robs us of life.

I've often wondered if Baden Powell, who formed the scouts, ever read the story of the ten virgins when he coined the phrase 'Be Prepared'. If you look in Matthew 25 you can read all about them. These girls are waiting for an important person, their bridegroom! But half of them don't plan ahead and run out of their necessary stuff, and miss out on the ball, Cinderella… or something like that (go read it later). Anyway girls, the point of the story is if we are going to be women of destiny we have to get our act together. We need to take responsibility for how we plan our time and execute our responsibilities. All of us have 24 hours in each day and it's up to us how we use the time.

Ministries, accomplishments, events, big deals… all take preparation. There is no short cut. We can look at great things and be fooled into thinking it was easy when the truth is it was probably hard work and a lot of planning. We will accomplish very little without a plan and babe, to be women of vision we need a plan. I want to challenge you today to think about where you'd like to be this time next year. How are you going to get to where you need to be? Are there things you'll need to give up and others things you need to develop in order for that goal to be reached? What strategies are you going to use to get there?

At the moment I'm studying psychology as I believe God wants to use that to further His kingdom, so I'm preparing the ground for that to happen. But I've gotta be real with you, it's bloomin' hard work and I often feel overwhelmed by the academia of it all. Preparation is simply hard work and if we're going to achieve anything it will require hard work… I know that sucks!

Like those wise virgins we need to be prepared and plan for the way ahead. Babe, you can achieve so much…pray it through, plan it out, then go for it… YOU GOT THE POWER!

Proverbs 3 v 6 "*In all your ways acknowledge the Lord and He will direct your paths.*"
Proverbs 15 v 22 *"Plans fail for lack of counsel [preparation], but with [careful consideration] advice they succeed"*
Proverbs 16 v 3 "*Commit to the Lord whatever you do and your plans will succeed.*"

Drop 82 ~ Don't buy the lie!

If you only knew how I struggle with a lack of confidence and self-doubt at times. Even as I write this book I'm bombarded with little negative voices in my head telling me I have nothing of worth to say, and who do I think I am anyhow! This is the voice of the father of lies, because all of us have something of value to say. My friend asked me one day how she could identify the voice of the Father against the voice of the destroyer. I told her, "The Father's voice always brings forth life, there's creativity even in the challenges, but creative life nonetheless. The destroyer's voice will always have death in some form. It may be self pity, rebellion, pride or despair but death in some form will be in it."

Do you know what… we can only ever know who we are when we allow God to tell us through His word? When we learn the truth off by heart so that we can whip it out like a pistol from our knickers towards the attacker… The devil hates us to know God's word because it protects us and renders him impotent towards us. By proclaiming the truth of who you are when you feel least like it, you can change how you feel. Truth will win over feeling every time if you can discipline yourself to get the Bible out and actually speak to your spirit when you least feel like it. I wonder, who do you think you are…?

Q. Who are you?

A. You are cherished and chosen, called by name child, you are the loved beyond measure son/daughter of the King! {Gal 4 v 7} {1 Peter 2 v 9}
You are a disciple of Christ and are entrusted with the keys of the kingdom of Heaven. {Matt 16 v 19}
You are more than a conqueror and will gain in all surpassing victory in all things through Christ. {Romans 8 v 37}

Q. Why are you?

A. You are predestined and chosen before time to be united with Christ in love, and accomplish the plans and purposes of God. {Ephesians 1 v 4 & 5} You are a mighty force upon this earth! {2 Chron 7 v 14}

Q. How are you?

A. You are blessed and forgiven. {Psalm 32 v1}
You are favoured in God's eyes, strong and certain of His blessing to you. {Proverbs 3 v 4}

Q. What are you?

A. You are controlled by the love of Christ. {2 Cor 5 v 14}

You are a person of faith and belief and will be rewarded for seeking Him. {Hebrews 11 v 6}

Oh, the capacity we have to forget these truths is amazing! Girlfriend...if God says we are all of the above and more and we know it's impossible for Him to lie, then it's not hard to work out who the liar is! Next time you hear those little negative voices, take out your own special verses and kick his ass! X x x

James 4 v 7 *"Submit yourselves then, to God. Resist the devil and he will flee from you."*

Footnote: why not learn one of the above off by heart...stick it on your bathroom mirror and memorise it and be encouraged when you brush your teeth!

Drop 83 ~ Eggshell shuffle

I used to try and please people because I was told a submissive servant heart was a thing I should demonstrate if I was a 'real' Christian. I'd never admit to disagreeing with anyone's view point and I'd really try to keep my thoughts to myself; which is cool, because well… you don't wanna know some of my thoughts! However we were not created to tip toe through life. There is a danger of so wanting to keep everybody happy that we walk on eggshells just in case we offend anyone. Honey bun, the "eggshell" shuffle of life is exhausting…! When we seek to keep everyone happy we allow a collection of people shape our identity rather than God. This is awful because you were made in His image and likeness,[1] you're meant to be crafted and shaped by Him alone. Only His loving hands are qualified for this. Sweetie pie, don't allow fear of other people to define you, it'll be a botch job, I assure you! Just look at the fragile ego of any celebrity!

When you're walking on eggshells for fear of breaking them, you can't walk in creativity because creativity and fear don't mix. I once worked for a person who was explosive and aggressive. This made for a poor working environment, where we, the staff would tiptoe around the place. After that boss had left I noticed I still did my job in the shadow of fear. You see the problem with learning to walk on eggshells is that one day when they are taken away, you can still tip toe about as if they're still there. Not good, huh?

In Christ we are free to stomp around in big beautiful blessed boots! When we know Jesus as our saviour and best friend we can enjoy the fact that we walk this journey out on solid ground. Are any areas in your life where you still feel like you're walking on eggshells? Ask the Holy Spirit to show you then let Him to take you by the hand and restore your confidence.

Princess, allow God to shape you, to mould you and place His mark upon your character. I really want to encourage you to walk in humility and boldness, trusting and praising God for who you are when surrendered to Him. If we're going to be productive for the Kingdom, babe, you're gonna have to get used to breaking a few '*ego*' shells and praise God for having a few of your own crushed in the process! Next time it rains go stomp in some puddles and remind yourself you're free!

Jeremiah 18 v 4 *"So I went down to the potter's house and saw him working at the wheel. But the pot he was shaping from the clay was marred in his hands; so the potter formed it into a new pot, shaping it as seemed best to him."*

Drop 84 ~ We've all got a part in this band!

In an orchestra, there are loads of different sections, all with a time and method of playing. There are many components… the brass section might be big, loud, up front and, well… brassy! The string section might give flow and feeling. The wind section, well enough said! Anyway what I'm trying to get at is that church either locally or globally, is a bit like an orchestra. All of us have an instrument to play, and a time to play it. We need to be sensitive to the rest of the orchestra and practise with what we've been given if we're going to enhance the sound.

We have a responsibility to serve and serve well the rest of those God has called us to make sweet music with… focusing on our contribution to the overall sound and not simply our own triangle or shaker! Ask yourself these questions about your own band… How in tune am I? Am I working with a desire to harmonise or cause discord? Am I in the right section for my gifting, personality? You see princess, we can only change ourselves, work on our own particular instrument, practise and perfect the flaws in our own unique performance.

There should be no Prima Donna's in this orchestra, rather each member looking to enhance the others' performance. But the choice to slot in and take your place is done because you long to please the conductor and give recognition or glory to the genius of the composer. Our goal is simply to make the orchestra the best we can by our little contribution. You can be at the back or the front, it doesn't matter just as long as you're there. Your role is valuable and the group needs you to play your part because you make a beautiful sound. Like an orchestra, it only works because everyone plays together.

If you are unsure of what you should be doing why not get involved in some practical aspects of your church? Dishes always need washed and people always need lovin'…

Honey, this is some orchestra… and you've got a drum to bang, so go play, go enjoy, you sound great!

Psalm 150 v 3-6 *"Praise Him with the sounding of the trumpet, praise Him with the harp and lyre, praise Him with tambourine and dancing, praise Him with the strings and the flute, praise Him with the clash of cymbals. Let everything that has breath, praise the Lord!"*

Drop 85 ~ The calling card of fear and shame

Hebrews 12 v 2&3

"Let us fix our eyes on Jesus, the author and perfecter of our faith, who for the joy set before him endured the cross, scorning its shame, and sat down at the right hand of God. Consider him who endured such opposition form sinful men, so that you will not grow weary and lose heart."

Consider for a moment the line from this verse, 'scorning its shame'. The Oxford dictionary cites the word 'scorn' as "to feel or show strong contempt for something unworthy". Christ, when He endured the price of our sin scorned the instrument of that punishment. He was the only one who could truly do this. He in turn allows us to set our shame at the foot of His cross in repentance and scorn the work of sin in our lives.

Girls I've done a lot in my life I'm not proud of, I have much to feel the sting of regret and shame over. Perhaps you too have areas of your past which make you cringe. Beloved the past is in the past. When you have repented and turned from sin you can, with freedom and certainty set its shame down and know you are pure and spotless regardless of how you feel!

Beth Moore says "shame is the calling card of the devil". I think that is so wise, when you feel ashamed you can be certain you've had activity in your life by one of his troops. Shame leaves a bad after taste in the mouth keeping us reminded in fear that someday, someone might just find you out. Shame keeps us in the fear that what was left behind will catch us up and destroy all our efforts of righteousness and the newness of creation in Christ. Trust me babe, shame is not from God…

Next time you have that sinking feeling in the pit of your stomach and fear or shame pulls you down, don't try and justify yourself or come up with excuses. Instead bless yourself in the knowledge that you are a new creation. You are a new creation in each moment of the day; indeed we are only ever as good as we are in <u>this</u> moment. Rejoice because Jesus died on the cross and rose again and gives us a new start in Him, we get to wipe the slate clean and move forward from our mistakes with the goal to learn from them and grow. So… if you find yourself with a calling card you don't want, chuck it in the bin! Today is a new day…. And you are a princess!

2 Corinthians 5 v 17 "*Therefore, if anyone is in Christ, he is a new creation; the old has passed away and the new has come!*"

Beth Moore, "Living Beyond Yourself" (DVD session 5) course number CG-0477 Life way publishing Nashville Tennessee 2005.

Drop 86 ~ Invest in yourself

Learning about God stuff takes time and energy, but every single thing you do to develop in Christ is like an investment into your spiritual bank account. It's never wasted and so worth it... In the West we are blessed with so many fabulous ways to invest in our spirit. Some of the conferences I go to are amazing, it's a privilege to go and a genuine recharge to the old batteries! To all of you who work hard to run these kinds of events I salute you! There are wise teachers and courses you can go to, in order to develop in understanding all the God stuff. The worship music we can buy on the high street truly rocks! And there are champions who break new ground so the rest of us get to swim in the slip stream. We are richly resourced to go deeper into God. I love this because the next generation is being confronted with a lot of stuff which requires Godly wisdom and courage.

Girlfriend, be inspired to make a deposit in yourself today. Get God into you life in as many areas as you can. Listen to sermons on your way to work (obviously not boring ones you might fall asleep and crash the car!). Stick bible verses which encourage you round your house remind yourself whose child you are. Memorise a bit of the bible which is special to you; bind it to your heart like a precious treasure and one day you'll be glad you did. Beloved all these things are ways of investing in the eternal you. These body's we're in are temporary and will one day pass way, but the soul will live forever. The one commodity we're all equal on is time so I reckon it'll matter to our eternal self how we spend it. The bible tells us to store up treasure for ourselves in Heaven where neither moth nor rust can harm it.[1]

You are worth investing in; remember God sees all those iddy biddy steps of faith, love or sacrifice. He sees and He cares as you try and unpack life in His direction. He delights in teaching us developing us as we journey through time. So next time you stop at the traffic lights and you're singing your head off to the latest Hillsongs c.d. smile, because your richer in God's kingdom because of your warbles! Find which strategies work for you in drawing you closer to God and implement those into your world.

Pat your own back that you've taken time to read this book and know you're a little bit richer for the reading...hopefully?

"Everybody lives forever...somewhere" (bumper sticker)

[1]Luke 12 v 33

Drop 87 ~ The Incredibles

Hunny bun you are Incredible… Together we are even more incredible and I think that rocks! I'm passionate that it is this divine inspired interaction which shapes history and changes the world. In short we need to cheerlead, invest and champion one another on in the journey. Today in this one day which you'll never have again, how are you going to be? How will you influence other people in this day, today? You have the power within your wonderful self - to egg on, inspire, encourage, support and arouse a whoop whoop! In this day!

Before your feet hit the floor, you can motivate yourself with something like, "Praise you God for this new day, thank-you for the freshness of it, help me be the best for you that I can be and take me deeper into you." I've found by doing this I can start with a more positive attitude and even on days where I'm battling with depression, I find it may not change how I feel right away, but it changes my position. It changes where I'm standing, because I position myself in the victory spot.

When I start my conscious day with an attitude of gratitude it releases perspective and it places me in a sense of security where feelings aren't my driving force; while it may not take away all the feelings, it declares the truth. And the truth will set you and me free! We're incredible regardless of how we may feel; Heaven declares it and Hell knows it!

When we are able to embrace who we truly are in Christ we can live in the freedom from all the stuff that holds us back. We can often be our own obstacles to living in freedom, because we're afraid to try something different or we tell ourselves 'I can't'. Hunny bun, when was the last time you tried something new? When was the last time you went out of your way to encourage someone? God is so creative and I believe he wants us to embrace the joy of incredible living not just going through the motions. Tell yourself 'I can!' Speak words of encouragement to yourself, hold tight to His truth and reject the lies of the enemy. You are able to do more than you think you can, but taking that first step is the hardest part. Often the greatest obstacle to an amazing life is ourselves! Step out babe…

YOU ARE INCREDIBLE….!

Philippians 4 v 13 "I *can do all things through Christ who strengthens me."*

Drop 88 ~ Danger, God squad @ work!

I'm Irish, us lot have a tendency to call a spade a spade. But hey, the truth even about spades is that they will set you free or something like that.... Anyway talking of tools, I was thinking about us, because we are the tools God uses to build His church. God's tools aren't big and flash they are often quite broken. They may not have the latest technology or most streamline of management, but they are useful in the hands of the master. I go to a very ordinary church, which has people from all walks of life which is brill. However because God like Bertie Basset, uses all sorts, sometimes we'll make a bit of a mess of things...and inadvertently cause wee frustrations.

So what do we do when you do when frustrated by the God squad...? Well hun, the first thing I'd suggest is that you stay put, remember your leaders are also on a journey and there is no such thing as a perfect church! Be honest with yourself about your frustrations, is there perhaps an element of pride involved? PRAY for your church, pray for the direction it's going – yes babe that is totally our responsibility! Position yourself; because if you are determined to be productive and the attitude of your heart is right you will be.

Position yourself...

- deeper in the word, pull it apart, discuss it, use it.
- in the centre of the work not on the fringes.
- around positive talk refuse to speak/listen to gossip or negativity.
- around people who are 'HOT' with passion for the Lord who will inspire you.
- in obedience, thy will thy way - not mine!
- in faith – greater is the power behind you than the task ahead of you!!!

Know that all God needs is a heart surrendered to Him and He'll do the rest. I've found is that when I dig deeper into God other people see new life in me and together we strengthen each other. Girlfriend we are always stronger together so strive for harmony and unity because it there that God commands His blessing. You may never see the fruit of baking a pie, you may never know how your gracious behaviour inspired hope, but determine to bring Glory to God and you will be used. I have seen this principle at work in my own life...and it does work, honestly! Hang on in there because you're probably more effective than you realise.

Proverbs 16 v 3 “Commit to the Lord whatever you do and your plans will succeed”. Go look up verse 9!

Drop 89 ~ Fruit or phew!

John 15 v 16 *"You did not choose me but I chose you and appointed you to go and bear fruit - fruit that will last...."*

God is so mind blowing in the simplicity of His wisdom when it comes to fruit and gifts. He has placed within you something amazing (it probably doesn't feel that amazing to you, more like second nature) but He has placed a unique gift within you. We each have things which no one else can do, big things and small things but all important. I was thinking about how we're meant to bear fruit, fruit that will last and God showed me the big fruit bowl in my kitchen. Our gifts are meant to be shared; they have no power until they are shared for another's benefit.

I can sing, from the age of five, the nuns at my school taught me and I loved it! But it's not until I bless others with my harmonies or tunes that my gift bears fruit. Yes I can use my voice to sing in the shower, but that blesses no one and annoys my teenage children particularly when they've got friends over (*which is kinda fun?*). However, back to the analogy! I need to bring my wee fruit to the banqueting table of the Lord and share it with others if I am to bless and be fruitful. What is your gifting - if you really can't think of anything, ask God to show you. I firmly believe we are all good at something! How can you use your unique gift to bless others?

1 Cor 7 v 7 "*...Each one has their own gift from God; one has this gift another has that..."*

By using our talents, driving, brain surgery, elbow rubbing or kick boxing - *ok possibly not the best example but whatever* - to bless, we release a flow of fresh blessing. If we hoard our gift away, not only will it bear no fruit it is likely to stagnate and go crusty! If I never sang, my vocal chords would lose muscle and tone and it's the same with your gifting; you've got it to use it! Fruit stored away in a cupboard will eventually go off, phew!

Better to leave it out in full view in a big bowl to be shared and enjoyed.

Go and read 1 Corinthians 12 and see if it inspires what you place in your fruit bowl today.

Drop 90 ~ **<u>The Point...</u>**

Well done, princess, you have reached the end of this wee bit of your journey. I use the term journey because I hope you've found some new and interesting things within the blurb that is this book. But do ya know what...every journey you'll ever go on has a point and this is no different. There's a reason and the point to this book. My hearts desire is to communicate this journey in a real way. People are real and need other 'real' people to communicate the love of Christ. If we huddle in some wee club of shared common ideas we've totally missed the point of our mandate. The world watches on as we walk our walk. Are you walking in your own shoes, being the best you, you can be? Do you leave a trail of fragrant blessing?

I pray you can understand your awesome potential when you embrace who God has made you to be and go for Him with passion. I hope you are inspired and encouraged to overcome life's inevitable obstacles *('cos life is full of them)* and find God on the other side waiting to catch you as you step in faith. Girlfriend, if He says you can do it then trust Him, you can!

I want to encourage you not to stay in the shallows. We can kind of play at our relationship with God and keep Him at arm's length. I want to encourage you to trust Him because there is so much more to behold when you dive into the depths of knowing Him. He is totally trustworthy and is always motivated by your best interests even when that seems impossible. He is totally faithful and His love unlike human love is totally pure in its selflessness.

The last point...? Enjoy the journey; gosh Christians can be so anal...! Choose to be around those who make you laugh till you pee your pants! Choose to smile, to fragrance each day and be a joy carrier. Know your times are in His hands if you surrender them to Him. Take time to push on and press through towards your goal in that season. Take time to rest, take time to heal, take time to love and enjoy being loved in new ways everyday.

Now go...be FABULOUS DARLING, you rock and the world is waiting for you!

It's Your Turn Now!

I feel truly humbled to have had the privilege of input into your world through this book, I pray that you've been encouraged and blessed. I don't know your circumstances but I know a man who does... His name is Jesus and He sits at the right hand of the Father in Heaven exacting purpose through the Holy Spirit. He'd be thrilled to hear from you because you were born to be in sweet union with Him. If you don't know Him and want to why not pray the prayer on the last page... it's over to you...

If you do know Him and want to go deeper, start with prayer... I've found the following helpful...

Get practical:

1) How can you build God-time into your day?
2) What are your strengths, how can you develop these?
3) What needs are in front of you which you could practically meet as you remember you are not Mother Teresa, are you? (Cook a meal, give a lift, send a card?)
4) What are your dreams? What plans do you need to put in place to achieve those dreams?
5) Who do you know who is going hard after the things of God... how can you learn from them?

If you don't know Him you might wanna pray this prayer...

"Dear God,
I realise I don't really know you, but I want to. I know there is sin in my life, which holds me back from you and I humbly ask that you'd come into my life and start your healing cleansing process through the power of your Holy Spirit. I thank you that you sent your Son, Jesus to die for me and because He died and rose again I have this opportunity to change my life. I no longer want to do things my way and surrender to your way so I can now live and walk with you as my friend. I trust and thank you that you have heard this prayer and I believe you will be faithful to me. Take my hand and take my life so we can start our journey. Amen."

(If you've prayed this prayer, may I be the first to welcome you to the family of believers, princess!) Now go tell someone... Yahoo!!!